AF445723

Source: Carlos Parks, "Gird Up Your Mind", 2024, "Used with permission."

Gird Up Your Mind

Living with Mental Illness

Nikki Collier

Contents

Dedication

I dedicate this book to everyone who has, will, or are struggling with mental illness. Whether it's themselves or someone they know and love, I hope my story shows that there is light at the end of the tunnel.

I also dedicate this to my husband, Eric, for always being there and standing by my side through it all. Thank you for your unconditional love, despite my faults. You have provided a wonderful life for me and our two beautiful children. I would be remiss if I did not mention my appreciation for your constant sacrifice and your genuinely kind heart. I love you so much.

To my children—Tim and Trinity, I am proud of the young man and woman you have become. I admire your tenacity and fortitude. Keep moving forward in your endeavors knowing you can do all things through Christ who strengthens you. Know that I will always love and support you.

Acknowledgements

To my mom—Linda Peters, you have been the wind beneath my wings. Thank you for loving me during the best and worst of times and supporting whatever I wanted to do. Constantly there to lend an ear and give direction and wisdom, you have helped me navigate through this thing called life. For always giving so much of yourself to improve my life and make it easier, I love you for the unconditional love you've provided to not just me, but the entire family. You truly are the glue to our family, making anytime we get together so special.

To Richard Peters—You are responsible for me being the well-rounded and confident person I am today. You have given me a great appreciation for the outdoors by exposing me to so many things dealing with nature. I appreciate your staunch support over the years. You have been a great father-figure and role model for me. Thank you for loving me as your own. I love you for the love you've shown not only to my mother, but to me and my family as well.

To my biological father—You are part of the reason I am breathing. While we have not had lots of moments together, know that I cherish the memories we've shared. I hope we can make many more before we both leave this earth.

To my sister—Heather you have been such a joy. We do not get to spend as much time together as I would like, (due to distance) but we always make up for lost time when we see each other. Thanks for being a great sister and an outstanding auntie to my children.

To my "getaway girls"—You know who you are (most of whom I have known since the sixth grade). Over the years, I've enjoyed our times of fellowship and how we encourage each other to press forward in making our goals and dreams become reality. I love how we always have each other's backs and I thank God that our paths crossed; I love you all.

To Pastor R. Kevin Matthews and First Lady Malissa Matthews—Thank you for your stewardship over your flock. I appreciate the teachings, love, support, and guidance you provide to me and other members of The Shepherd's House International Christian Church. This Bible-based church has taught me, and countless others "How to Study the Bible for Yourself." I'm thankful that you took a leap of faith and established this five-generational church where we are, "Caring for people, Equipping people for destiny, and Preparing people for eternity."

To Pamela Love Manning, PhD—Thank you for offering that I carpool with you to the Masterlife class every week. Little did I know this connection would propel me to write this book. Not only did you mentor me, but you inspired me to follow in your footsteps by becoming an author. Your course, "Writing and Self-Publishing Your Book," has been invaluable. You have taught me I can be a finisher too and, as you say, "Finishers make progress, not excuses!" You have walked this path ahead of me, so your advice and insight have been immeasurable. Thanks for keeping me accountable. At last, I can now say out loud, "I am a FINISHER!"

To Cathy Price—My coach, thanks for keeping me on task and encouraging me on the importance of self-care and having balance in my life. I appreciate you.

To Andrea L. Reid—My editor, thank you for causing me to dig deeper and confront personal and unresolved issues from my past. Writing this book proved to be therapeutic, as it became part of my healing process. I also appreciate your devotion to making sure the reader gains a better understanding of mental illness and its impact on others.

To Jackie Hicks—Portrait artist and owner of Fond Memories Photography, thank you for capturing beautiful pictures of me. I absolutely love your work!

To Kym Lee—Your makeup artistry is amazing, and I thank you for making me look beautiful with your talent.
To Carlos Parks—My cousin, thank you so much for your art and for understanding the purpose and importance of this book.

To my book club buddies—Delois Pearsall and Wakeya Belt, also aspiring authors, I appreciate the level of accountability we showed to each other during our writing process. I'm excited for both of you, and I look forward to reading your books!

To Dr. Jonathan Shepherd—Thank you for writing the foreword to this book and for your expertise in the mental health profession.

To Dr. Ennis—Thank you for your listening ear over the years as I navigated the trials of life.

To Max Manning, PhD—Thank you for teaching the class, "God's Plan for Your Life: Vision and Destiny," where you "help people see further than they can look" and for linking me up with my current Christian therapist. You know who you are—you have been the best thing ever at this point in my life.

I especially want to honor the late Minister Steve Dory for sparking my interest in screen writing through his screen writing class at our former church. Whenever he saw me in passing, he'd always ask how my book was coming along. A gentle giant, I'm also thankful he was able to capture my wedding ceremony so beautifully on video. He will be missed by many. Until we meet again, rest in peace.

There are so many others to recognize, but the list is already too long. Though your names may not be listed, know that I love and appreciate all of you as well.

Foreword

King Solomon in The Holy Bible is recognized as one of the wisest persons to live on the face of the earth. Many of his signature writings provided guidance through life's challenges and can be found in the books of Proverbs and Ecclesiastes. Such sayings include, "A good name is better than precious ointment; send your grain across the seas, and in time, profits will flow back to you; and to everything there is a season, and a time to every purpose under the heaven." However, there is one area that even King Solomon found difficult to tackle in his writings: when an individual's life experiences are different from the desired expectations.

As a practicing board-certified child, adolescent, and adult psychiatrist, one of the most heart-wrenching situations to face is the announcement of a newly diagnosed mental health disorder to an individual due to behaviors and responses that are out of line with reality. Such an announcement can be devastating for both the person and the person's family because there is a realization that the dreams and goals once desired may no longer be in reach because of this new twist in the person's life journey. Being diagnosed with a medical condition can be a game changer for any person, but even more so when the diagnosis is a psychiatric illness. Questions such as What's wrong with me? Am I weak-minded? Or am I crazy? will crowd the mind and thoughts and potentially stagnate a person into a season of unproductivity due to worry, doubt, hopelessness, and worthlessness.

I am thrilled that Nikki Collier chose to pen this unprecedented view into her life, in "Gird Up Your Mind," to address the responses needed when a person's experiences do not line up with the person's expectations. Nikki's transparency about her own mental health challenges is refreshing; yet sobering at the same time. As you read her story, allow the testimonials to penetrate your heart and revitalize your will to fulfill your assigned dreams and goals despite the season you find yourself in. To "gird up your mind" means to equip yourself mentally and emotionally with the necessary tools and resources to get back into the ring and fight for your desired outcomes in life. The book, "Gird Up Your Mind," is one of these necessary tools and resources.

It is my privilege and pleasure to endorse this book for your enjoyment and enlightenment. For those who find themselves in an unproductive season, remember the verses in Ecclesiastes chapter 5: "It is a good thing to receive wealth from God and the good health to enjoy it. To enjoy your work and accept your lot in life — this is indeed a gift from God. God keeps such people so busy enjoying life that they take no time to brood over the past."

–Jonathan Shepherd, M.D., FAPA, DFAACAP

Endorsements

Interweaving her story with practical suggestions, Nikki Collier takes the reader on her life's journey that begins in despair but achieves fulfillment through treatment and the power of faith. Whether you are trying to understand bipolar disorder or searching for a path to healing, this book will teach you how to gird up when life becomes challenging or confusing.

–Judy Haran, Ph.D., LCSW-C

First and foremost, I want to congratulate my dear friend and former co-worker, Nikki Collier, for undertaking this assignment. The courage and transparency bring to life the trials, emotional struggles and esteem issues that can surface in the life of those who suffer from any form of mental illness. Having personally experienced it because of a family member, I know the devastating impact it can have not only on the one who has been diagnosed, but also the circle of family and friends who are also affected. Nikki, thank you for your willingness to tell your story and hopefully, in doing so, tell someone else, who like you have had to deal with these issues, that they too can make it!

–Minister Lee Michaels, Retired Morning Show Host and
Program Director for WCAO Heaven 600

In this engaging book, Nikki exposes you to a part of her life story that has caused her (and others) pain and frustration, but also joy and peace. Her transparency and vulnerability will not only help you look at people with mental illness differently but encourage you to appreciate the strength and resilience of people you've labeled, misjudged, or misunderstood.

–Pam Love, PhD, Author, Coach, Pres. of DP Love Enterprises
and Founder of the Finishers Network

Introduction

"Peace I leave with you, my peace I give unto you: not as the world giveth, give I unto you. Let not your heart be troubled, neither let it be afraid." – John 14:27 (KJV)

Being diagnosed with bipolar disorder is difficult to accept because it solidifies that you have a mental illness. Dealing with this revelation can cause anyone to exhibit all kinds of feelings. Fear is an emotion that can kick in quickly. Various thoughts can circulate in one's mind. How will people treat me if they become aware of my condition? Will they look at me like I'm crazy? Will they treat me like a leper? These are some thoughts that plagued my mind.

My intention in writing this book and telling my story, my truth, is to bring awareness to this disorder. We have heard of celebrities who have been diagnosed with bipolar disorder: Patty Duke, Jenifer Lewis, Carey Fisher, Mariah Carey, Kanye West, and Demi Lovato, just to name a few. Well-known fashion icon Kate Spade committed suicide, followed by Celebrity Chef Anthony Bourdain. The world was stunned when famous country singer Naomi Judd committed suicide a day before being inducted into the Country Music Hall of Fame. Stephen "Twitch" Boss of the Ellen DeGeneres Show was also a casualty of suicide. The announcement that this seemingly cheerful guy took his own life sent shockwaves across the world. It seemed these individuals were living their best lives, yet they suffered internally, hiding their pain until some could take it no longer and elected to end their lives. Mental illness is a real issue that should not be overlooked or ignored because many people are suffering in silence.

I wrote this book because I thought it would be good to share the effects of mental illness from an ordinary person's perspective. While I have managed mine well over the years, there are many who wrestle with this sickness daily. By sharing my story, I strive to offer real transparency of what this disorder can do and how it can wreak havoc on our lives and the ones we love—who watch helplessly on the sidelines. But as I paraphrase what my best friend stated so eloquently to me, "You are a successful ordinary person and through perseverance, bipolar is manageable like any other illness. Despite your illness, you have built a beautiful life." If I can accomplish this, so can you. Bipolar disorder does not have to limit you and what you want out of life.

Chapter 1

A Time to Lose

As I looked through my senior high school yearbook, there was no trace of the life-changing senior ski trip my friend and I went on. The details of the day are a blur to me as I don't remember the exact date when we took the trip, nor do I recall packing for the trip or riding the bus to the ski resort in Pennsylvania. All I remembered was feeling increasingly paranoid. I remembered feeling like people were trying to poison me. The next thing I knew, I was having a panic or anxiety attack, which was what my teacher/chaperone called it. I don't know what came over me, but I experienced shortness of breath and could not breathe. I literally could not catch my breath—it was like I was hyperventilating. When it happened, I was lying on the bottom bunk bed in the ski chalet. My best friend tried to reassure me that what I was thinking was not the case. The paramedics eventually came and took me out on a stretcher to the hospital. From there, they must have called my parents, who came and picked me up and brought me home.

The ride home with my parents was pretty foggy and I don't really remember what I said to them as we drove home, but I knew my parents were concerned about me. When I arrived home, I felt the need to sterilize my things—mainly toiletries—in hot water in my bathroom sink. I believe that was the last straw for my mom because the next thing I knew; I was at the hospital. She admitted me into a psychiatric ward, and I stayed there I believe, for one week and then had to stay another week at home. This caused me to miss two weeks of school during my senior year. What I remembered the most from the stay in the psychiatric ward was that my biological father visited me with my younger sister. This was etched in my mind because I did not see him very often and I had never seen my sister before then. She was from another marriage, so it was good seeing her for the first time. My biological father just visited that one time, but my mom visited me every day. Aside from that, what I remembered about being in the ward was (again) a blur because I was so medicated and out of it.

I don't recall what I said or what I thought when my mom informed me they diagnosed me as being Bipolar I. She mentioned that I said little and that it was probably something I thought would eventually go away. My parents were trying to learn how to help me manage my condition, ensure my breakdown did not happen again, and that I complied with taking my medication. I didn't exactly know all of what it entailed being labeled as bipolar, but I knew I did not want that to be the case.

According to the American Psychiatric Association (APA), bipolar disorders are considered "brain disorders that cause change in a person's mood, energy, and ability to function." The National Alliance on Mental Illness (NAMI) says, "Bipolar Disorder is broadly defined as a cycle of manic and depressive episodes, but there are actually three different types." These types are Bipolar I, Bipolar II, and Cyclothymic. People with bipolar disorders generally have periods of normal moods as well. This condition can be treated and getting late. Let's clean the shit up and dispose of the trash. I, for one, would like a hot meal and a drink. We'll head out at first light to finish off the rest of the Vipers."

A few hours later, I have Alba sitting on my lap while we all sit around, enjoying a drink and watching the kids as they finish decorating the massive Christmas tree placed in the center of the room. "Val, stop eating the decorations," Alba laughs as our daughter devours the garland made from popcorn. Val giggles, then runs and climbs into Leyna's lap.

"I'm hungry." Gabe pops another kernel in his mouth.

"That boy is always eating." Alba sighs, then rubs at her belly.

"You okay, Mi Amor?"

"Yeah. The baby is very active tonight." She takes hold of my hand and places it where hers is resting. I feel my lips lift at the corners, feeling the movement of our unborn child.

"Mommy, can I listen?" Gabe comes running up to us, carrying the small at-home fetal doppler Emerson gave us.

Alba smiles at our son. "Sure, sweetheart." Alba takes the monitor, lifts her sweater enough to expose her pregnant belly, and moves it around until the steady rhythm of our baby's heartbeat echoes. Alba turns the volume up a bit, and Gabe lays his head against his momma's belly. The chatter stops, and the room falls silent. The only other noises are little giggles from the younger kids playing with the train set circling the tree's base. The whooshing sounds capture almost everyone's attention, and the entire family listens.

I look across the room to where Val is nestled in my sister's lap, sleeping.

I feel content.

For a moment, all our troubles and worries fade.

"You could make this a lot less painful if you just tell us what we want to know." Jake leans back and folds his arms across his chest. "Your buddy there lasted longer than I expected." Jake jerks his head at the man lying on the floor, and the guy cuts his eyes at his dead brother. "If you're willin' to suffer, my man here is more than happy to accommodate you."

"Give it your best shot." The guy smirks, and I bring the wrench down a second time, crushing the kneecap of his other leg. Bored with the weapon in my hand, I toss it to the side. I step away and retrieve a nail gun. I don't wait for Jake to question him again. Instead, I step up to the biker's left hand and drive three nails into the palm of his hand, then casually stroll to the right and do the same to his other palm.

"Fuck!" he bellows in agony.

A rush of cold air swirls around my feet as the barn doors open. Reid steps inside. "I have a location," he says. "They're holed up in an abandoned cabin at the foothill of the mountain range north of Flathead."

"You sure?" Logan asks, and Reid looks at him.

"One of our sources spotted them less than an hour ago. He tracked them down to the location I just mentioned." Reid pauses when the fucker in my grasp opens his mouth and begins to laugh.

I turn my attention from Reid to the sorry son of a bitch and press the nail gun to his chest. I pull the trigger and drive a 2 ½ inch nail in his chest. His eyes widen. I lower the nail gun to the floor, and on my way up, pull a knife from my boot. I place the blade against his jugular, pausing long enough to look back at Jake. His sharp nod is the answer I need. I face the cocksucker one more time. *"Decirle al diablo que dije hola."* My blade slices through his flesh. Crimson soaks his cut, and he gurgles, choking on his blood. After a few more gasping breaths, life fades from his eyes.

"You've got style, brother." Quinn claps my back.

Jake stands. "We've been out here most of the damn day. It's people with these illnesses can lead full and productive lives. It should also be noted that bipolar disorder can run in families. Eighty to ninety percent of individuals with bipolar disorder have a relative with either depression or bipolar disorder. However, environmental factors can also contribute to bipolar disorder.

According to Dr. Ken Duckworth, the chief medical officer of the National Alliance on Mental Illness (NAMI), "Bipolar I disorder is characterized by manic episodes lasting at least a week or manic symptoms that often require immediate hospital care. The episodes of mania are typically followed by a period of depression. During manic or hypomanic episodes people may show symptoms like: unusually intense emotions, loss of appetite, decreased need for sleep, fast talking, racing thoughts."

Also, according to the National Institute of Mental Health (NIMH), "They may also report feeling up, high, jumpy or wired, more irritable or elated. People experiencing a manic episode may also believe they can do many things at once or feel they are unusually talented, important, or powerful." Additionally, "There may also be more risky behavior, such as excessive eating or drinking, reckless sexual activity and uncharacteristic spending." Furthermore, "Depressive episodes have near-opposite symptoms with people often experiencing: increased appetite, changed sleeping patterns, slowed down or restless, feeling sad, empty or helpless, may speak very slowly in conversation." NIMH also says, "People experiencing a depressive episode may have trouble concentrating and making decisions, take little interest in 'almost all activities' and can have thoughts of death or suicide. The APA also says sleeping too little or too much is a symptom of a depressive episode."

Dr. Ken Duckworth of NAMI also says, "Since bipolar disorder is relatively cyclical, episodes may be triggered by similar things, such as time changes or changes in seasons (due to changing amounts of sunlight)." According to the NIMH, "The condition is diagnosed during late adolescence or young adulthood. For women, bipolar may appear in pregnancy or postpartum. An estimated 4.4% of US adults experience bipolar disorder at some time in their lives." Moreover, "Bipolar II disorder is defined by a pattern of depressive episodes, followed by brief, hypomanic episodes. Hypomania is defined as a mild form of mania, marked by elation and hyperactivity. Hypomanic episodes are not as extreme as true manic episodes experienced in Bipolar I disorder, according to Duckworth, but have similar trademarks, such as impulsivity. The third type, Cyclothymia, is defined by periods of hypomanic symptoms and depressive symptoms lasting for at least two years (but lasting for at least one year in children)."

Looking back, I think a combination of culminating things that happened during my senior year made me snap while on that ski trip because I somehow lost touch with reality. I had broken up with my drug dealer boyfriend, whom I loved dearly (or so I thought). Well, he was not really a boyfriend, but he was the one I lost my virginity to. I thought I loved him and could not imagine a life without him. He was what we called back in the day, a "bad boy" and I was hooked on him. Add to that the fact that school stressed me out. I went to a Catholic high school where a lot was expected of me, and I expected a lot of myself as well. I was trying to balance a stringent program at school, had extra-curricular activities (I was President of the Spanish Club), applying to colleges, and tried to maintain a social life.

In life, it is taught that people should be well-rounded, but what's not taught is how to be well-balanced. Going back to school after all that I endured the day of the ski trip was rather difficult. I was gone for two weeks, which was a lot of time to miss from school. It was especially difficult because I had my breakdown in front of a lot of my classmates. I am sure they thought I was off my rocker. It was embarrassing, and I decided I would not explain to everyone who inquired about what happened. It was about this time when I realized who my genuine friends were. Thank God I had my best friend who was there with me when my breakdown occurred. She has been with me since we met in the sixth grade. I have four additional friends, most of whom I have known since the sixth grade, who have always had my back. I am thankful for them because they have never judged me and have always accepted me.

I survived my senior year, graduated, and then went off to college. But this was just the beginning of a lifelong struggle to come to terms with my diagnosis and the stigma associated with it. Fear perpetuates stigma because people do not know how to react to someone who is diagnosed as bipolar. In a Special Times Magazine Edition, "Mental Health A New Understanding" in an article, "Finding The Right Words" by David Bjerklie he states, "One of the most insidious and heartbreaking results of this stigma is that it discourages people from getting treatment." Bjerklie says in the beginning of his article, "Consider that question of fear. We are often afraid of people with mental disorders. We fear their unpredictability and our inability to fully comprehend their illness. We fear what looks like volitional behavior. A heart attack is not a choice when it's underway. A tumor can't be willed to disappear. But depression? Phobias? Anxiety? Obsessive-compulsive rituals? Buckle down. Get a grip."

These were valid points that Bjerklie made. There is a fear factor at play on the person with the disorder and those they encounter as different emotions and questions arise from both sides. People are uncomfortable because they do not know how to react to a person with a mental disorder. Some may expect those who struggle with anxiety, depression and other phobias to get themselves together. They may use words like whacky, weird, or out of their minds to describe those who have a mental disorder. Because they are unable to relate, the thought for those with the illness is to "Figure it out or work it out."

The fact is that people may feel uncomfortable because they don't understand the illness. With this in mind, those diagnosed with the illness may feel inadequate as well and have questions within themselves. The questions I struggled with were: Why me? How did I get to this point in my life? Will I always have to take medication to manage this bipolar disorder? Being a Christian since I was young, I wondered if this was something I could be totally healed and set free from, or would this be a thorn in my side that I would have to bear? Will I be able to live a happy and normal life? Those were some questions that swirled around in my head.

Bjerklie continued, "We also assume that if we reduce ignorance, we dispel stigma. Yet, studies have found that even when efforts to combat misconceptions are successful, the result is often that the tenacious underlying prejudices are merely exposed but remain in place. Most programs are built on the foundation that mental illnesses are like any other illnesses; the mistake comes in thinking that once people realize this, they will adopt a more accepting view. That's wishful thinking. Historic biases long ago made mental illnesses different, and they have remained that way in most people's perceptions. But surely the goal should be to educate the public that mental illnesses are brain disorders—real biological diseases—no matter what. Well, yes, and that has indeed become a pillar of education efforts for at least a generation."

When I heard people make comments like "she is so bipolar, or the weather is so bipolar, or I can't deal with him because he is so bipolar and all over the place," I always kept silent, but I always thought if they only knew the person they were speaking to was bipolar, they would be more careful with their choice of words. They carelessly threw words around casually, not giving any thought to how those words really affect those who are dealing with a mental disorder.

David Bjerklie further explained in the beginning of the article titled, "Finding The Right Words," where he stated, "Our words frame and reflect our understanding (and misunderstandings) about illness. But they also drive that understanding. Scary words elicit scary feelings; ugly words, ugly feelings. Words fuel stigma, but they can also protect, in ways we are just beginning to appreciate. Vocabulary matters… Now consider the words we use to describe the people who exhibit these symptoms. It's not just "crazy", "kooky", or "bonkers" which have little intrinsic meaning outside of their applications to mental illness. There are "cracked," "unhinged" and "unbalanced," words for a thing that is broken. There are "deranged," "unsound" and "berserk," …words that strip humanity entirely: the person who "goes ape," the person who is "batty." Imagine referring to a cancer patient as some kind of animal. We don't. We wouldn't. But the person with a mental illness? Sure."

"The National Alliance on Mental Illness in the U.S. has been particularly active in communicating the results of research on biological causes of serious mental illnesses. But that by itself doesn't solve the stigma problem… pushing this neurobiology model often reinforces "the belief that people will have no control over their behavior and that since the illness has affected the brain structure, they will not recover."

The statistical data previously mentioned is accurate. Knowing there is a stigma associated with those of us with bipolar or any other mental disorder can cause us to feel all kinds of emotions to cope with the diagnosis. I know for me, being diagnosed with a mental health disorder caused me great grief. However, I didn't realize I was grieving when I was diagnosed with Bipolar I. I tried to accept this as my new normal but how does one accept or process this new reality? I later realized I was experiencing the five stages of grief: denial, anger, bargaining, depression, and acceptance as I tried to process everything. Because of stigmas, having a mental disorder is not an easy road for many. For me, knowing people were going to place labels on me because of my diagnosis caused me great stress. I was in denial, was numb, and shocked at what was happening. I didn't want to accept this news as my new way of life. I wanted to believe it would go away, so I convinced myself to simply pretend it was not true and just ignore it all together. However, this was my life. Including meds in my daily plan or even therapy to help me cope was not what I envisioned for myself or my future. I just wanted to revert to the place before everything changed.

According to the Lung Foundation of Australia, "You may grieve the loss of your health, the loss of your identity and independence, or loss of future life plans." I also experienced anger and again asked, Why me? I wondered why I had to be hospitalized. Then I eventually transitioned into the bargaining phase. What could have been done to prevent this? What if certain traumatic situations did not happen, could I have avoided this? I concluded trauma can trigger bipolar disorder where it may not have ever surfaced. After that, I was depressed as the reality of it all set in for me. My depression lasted for quite some time. I would say for a few months. I sought therapy to help me cope and my therapist helped me to get to a place of acceptance—this diagnosis was real, and I had to learn how to manage it. I came to a place in my life where I had to learn to adjust to the labels and stigmas surrounding having a mental disorder. I gradually fought my way back.

The truth is, I cannot concern myself with what others may think or feel because I have enough to deal with in my life to let them and their labels define me. I turn to God to give me the strength I need to endure the effects of this disorder. What I knew was when I was at my lowest point, Emmanuel, "God with us," was there. He never left me, and I know I was never forsaken.

Chapter 2

A Time to Be Born

*"To everything there is a season, and a time to every
purpose under the heaven."*
– Ecclesiastes 3:1 (KJV)

My parents met when they were sophomores in college.
Interestingly enough, they were introduced by my biological father's
roommate who was dating my mother's roommate. On top of that, my
mom went to high school with both roommates. She explained that
she and my biological father dated for about two years while in college
and that he was in the ROTC program, which meant when he
graduated, he had to go to officers' training school in Oklahoma where
we later lived.

According to my mother, my Grandma Daisy purchased the
wedding rings for my parents to get married. My parents graduated
from college the same year I was born, but because of his military
obligations, unfortunately, my biological father could not witness my
birth because he was deployed to the U.S. Army on September 10,
1971. I was born prematurely because my mom had toxemia. She said
her blood pressure was extremely high, and that she had protein in her

11

urine. According to her, having this condition was dangerous to a mother and her child. And depending on its severity, toxemia can be fatal and must be monitored closely by a physician. She was in the intensive care unit overnight after I was born by C-section to monitor her blood pressure.

According to MedicineNet, "Toxemia: A condition in pregnancy, also known as pre-eclampsia (or preeclampsia) characterized by abrupt hypertension (a sharp rise in blood pressure), albuminuria (leakage of large amounts of the protein albumin into the urine) and edema (swelling) of the hands, feet, and face. Pre-eclampsia is the most common complication of pregnancy. It affects about 5% of pregnancies. It occurs in the third trimester of pregnancy. Pre-eclampsia occurs most frequently in first pregnancies and the initial treatment is bedrest and sometimes medication. If that becomes ineffective, the induction of labor and delivery or a C-section may have to be considered. Pre-eclampsia always resolves after a short time when the baby is born."

I was born on September 11, 1971, in Fort Meade, Maryland. My mother named me Nikki Joanne Holland, after famous poet, Nikki Giovanni who was one of her favorite poets. Not only that, Nikki is derived from the Greek root word, nikos. According to Rick Renner's *Sparkling Gems from the Greek*, "the word nikos describes an overcomer, a conqueror, champion, victor, or master. It is the picture of an overwhelming, prevailing force." Though I was born prematurely (I was due in October), my mother envisioned I would be strong and victorious in life.

Because my biological father was in training, he could not come home right away to see me. He eventually made his way home and was greeted with me as an early present. Per my mother, my father was excited to see me for the first time, especially since I looked so much like him. My Grandma Daisy came to see me, and according to my mom, she oohed and ahhed because I was the first-born child of her eldest son.

I spent my earlier upbringing as an infant on a military base in Oklahoma until about two years old and in Germany until I was about five years old. I spent kindergarten in Goldsboro, North Carolina, where my mother was from. We remained there for about a year and later moved to Fort Meade, MD, where we lived on the Fort Meade Military Base. This was where we were awakened by the Reveille Army Bugle wake-up call being played early every morning, generally around 7 a.m.

As a Second Lieutenant in the Army, my biological father was constantly on the go. As a child, I remembered more times being away from my father than with him. While his job afforded him the ability to take care of his family, it kept him away from us, so it came as no surprise when my parents separated when I was six years old. Evidently, I adjusted to the next phase of my life. Once they broke up and went their separate ways, I attended first through third grades in Odenton, Maryland. I remembered having a nice teenaged babysitter. She and her mom watched over me while my mom was at work. I admired her mom because she was a crossing guard and seeing her at work made me want to become a crossing guard as well. Crossing guards always caused us to feel safe while crossing the streets when we walked home from school. If anyone felt they were in danger, seeing homes with hand signs in the windows were indicators that those homes were safe havens for us to go to if we felt we were in danger.

The next move that we made was to Greenbelt, Maryland, where I attended Magnolia Elementary School, the third one that I attended. I was in the fourth grade by this time. This school provided a pretty good life for me because I made new friends and enjoyed playing with them outside—something kids don't do enough of nowadays. We knew to come home when the streetlights came on. We'd play hide and go get it (a version of hide and go seek) but I was always the good girl—no one was "getting" anything from me. As I grew older, the only thing I did that I knew my mom would not approve of was smoking with a friend. I remembered about the age of nine or 10 that we lived in an apartment and my friend and I were out on our balcony and decided to smoke a cigarette. My mom had lawn chairs out there and I somehow ended up burning a hole in her plastic lawn chair. So, what did I do? Cut that part out! I don't think she ever noticed.

I became what was called a latchkey kid after I complained about the people who were watching me at a so-called daycare. I saw them kick a child, but thankfully the only harsh punishment that was inflicted on me was having to stand in the corner. When I told my mom, she allowed me to stay home by myself. There was a neighbor across the hallway I could go to in case I needed anything.

A change came when my mom met a man through a good friend she knew in Germany. In fact, that friend and her husband knew my biological father. Her husband was in the fraternity with this man, the same fraternity my biological father was also a part of. This man would later become my father in every sense of the word. I didn't mind him coming by and seeing my mother. In fact, I thought it was nice having him around because he treated us so well. It was all good until I realized my mom catered to him by giving him special treatment whenever he visited for dinner. If he were coming over for the evening, she would set the table with the "good" silverware. She meticulously placed the food on the table so that it was a great presentation for him. But when it was just the two of us, we ate buffet style from the stove! I knew then he meant something to her. Looking back, he did a lot of nice things for us and introduced us to a lot of different things. I loved it when he purchased a goldfish tank for me, which was a smaller version of the big one he had in his apartment. This kind man spent quality time with me and often we'd go to the park and feed the pigeons. He also taught us how to water ski on his dad's boat and how to snow ski as well. He took me camping and became the dependable father I needed him to be.

Initially, the idea of him marrying my mother took some getting used to, but he grew on me. I accepted the fact that this man was going to be my mother's husband and my father. He was so good to us, which made it easy to accept and welcome him into our family. As the years went on, he really became my father in every way imaginable. I often felt bad whenever I lashed out at him in my anger. I knew yelling out to him, "You are not my dad!" was hurtful and not fair to him. But I was trying to accept the fact that it was not fair that my biological father was not living up to what I expected him to be.

We moved to Mitchellville, MD, and my mother and Pete finally married. The wedding day was spectacular! My mother was such a pretty bride. The wedding was small, intimate, and took place in our new home. Family and a few friends were in attendance, and it was perfect! It was around Christmas time and our home was nicely decorated. I was my mom's only bridesmaid, and I was so proud to wear the beautiful skirt she'd made for me to wear. I felt pretty in it and was delighted to wear it for her special day.

A part of the wedding that made me chuckle was when it was time to repeat the vows. I teased Pete because when it was time to say his vows he said, "I take thee Lindar to be my lawfully wedded wife." It tickled me because my mother's name is Linda, not Lindar. Their wedding was quaint and lovely. Pete made a handsome groom and my mom, just like the meaning of her name, (which means pretty in

Spanish), was simply beautiful. They decided to have a wedding like this to avoid spending a lot of money, since they had just purchased a new house. It was a gorgeous home, and I enjoyed visiting there. My mom told me when they were looking for it, I claimed my room in the house and Pete had not even asked her to marry him yet!

Now that our new residency was in Mitchellville, Md, it was where I attended my fourth and final elementary school, Ardmore Elementary. It was there that I met my dearest and closest friends. One friend I met at the bus stop when my mom dropped me off and asked her if I could stand with her. She seemed indifferent then, but we became close friends. After befriending each other, we rode our bikes together after school and on the weekends. She and I played spades all day at her house during the summer. Our parents even enrolled us into a computer camp, but we hated it and begged them to let us stay home instead. We ended up going to a basketball camp at the University of Maryland, College Park (Md) that I coaxed her into going with me. It was fun, but that alone did not help me make the basketball team in high school. Unfortunately, I did not put in enough time and practice; I didn't put in the work, therefore; I had to settle with being a statistician.

The kids in school were interesting but got on my nerves as well. There was a nasty boy in gym class who harassed me by making comments every time I bent over. He was such a jerk! This was one reason I wanted to go to an all-girls school. When I found out another one of my closest friends was going to the all-girls school, I told my mom I wanted to go too, and she allowed me to go. It was one of the best decisions of my life because it really prepared me for college and beyond.

I only mention these events of being harassed because, back in our day, what we called bullying was not as extreme as it is today. For one, we did not have social media back then. This technology has become a problematic bullying tool. Today's children are being bullied all the time—in person and on social media. A girl bullied my daughter in middle school, and it reached the point where my husband had to go up to the school to put an end to it. A meeting was held with him, my daughter, the girl (bully), her mother, and the assistant principal. It was beneficial because the girl stopped bullying my daughter. This bullying subconsciously had a psychological impact on her where she later struggled with her self-confidence and experienced other negative effects. I was thankful my husband put a stop to it.

Getting back to my younger days, I had a minor discomfort in middle school with being harassed and just getting adjusted to the school, but things improved once I got to high school. My high school years were great because I had my first job at an amusement park, had my first kiss and my first boyfriend in high school. Unfortunately, he left me for a close friend because I would not have sex with him; but she would. It was in my senior year that things changed drastically. This was where it all came to a head as I detailed a glimpse at the beginning of this book.

Chapter 3

A Time to Die

According to Merriam-Webster's Dictionary, the word die means "to cease functioning or to pass out of existence." The Free dictionary describes it as "experiencing an intense, seemingly unbearable reaction to something." I think both definitions describe what happened to me when I had the nervous breakdown or anxiety attack on my senior ski trip. You see, as I mentioned before, in my senior year, I got involved with a guy who was a drug dealer. We never went out on an official date because he lived within walking distance so that made it easy for me to sneak out to his house. My parents did not approve of him, of course, but that did not matter to me. I saw him any chance I could, despite their objections.

When I visited his house, we'd do some heavy petting, but we never had sex. One day, while we were making out, things got pretty heated and before I realized the gravity of the situation I was in, he attempted to take advantage of me and go all the way. The problem was that I had not decided I wanted to engage in a sexual experience with him. He continued despite me saying NO and asking him to stop.

19

I did not think of it as rape. All I knew was that I did not want it to go that far and did not know how to stop it once it started. I walked back home so shocked at what had happened that I shared with my mom. I didn't know what my mother was going to say or do, but I just remembered her listening and calming my fears.

Despite his uncaring behavior, I continued seeing him, allowing him to take advantage of my vulnerabilities. At some point, I realized he was no longer interested in me. I guess after he got what he wanted; he moved along. However, I became obsessed with him even though we were no longer seeing each other and were not really an item. I am sure he had another girl, and I found out later from his mom that he had a baby. I was so distraught because I could not accept the fact that I lost my virginity to him, and he did not reciprocate the same feelings toward me. I loved him (or so I thought). This was hard for me to handle, and then things went into a downward spiral.

Nobody saw it coming (I don't think)—I certainly didn't. But one of my high school friends told my mom something out of character that I said in religion class in response to questions being asked. In talking with her, now over 30 years later, she does not remember exactly what I said, but it must have been something to make her deeply concerned. My best friend said she recalled us having lunch in the cafeteria and that I was very anxious about colleges and college acceptances. And my mom said she almost did not let me go on the ski trip and planned on taking me to see a doctor when I returned home. Her concern or fear of what could possibly happen on the trip was realized when she received a phone call from the chaperone. She said the chaperone called her and asked what was wrong with me because of my behavior. After their discussion, they decided it was best to just send me to the hospital instead of keeping me at the ski chalet. My mom said the girls were upset because I accused them of poisoning me and talking about me. I was having an episode or crisis and had lost touch with reality.

While at the hospital, I remembered my biological father coming to visit me with my toddler sister and I was thrilled to see them. After coming out of this ordeal that lasted a week, I don't recall he and I ever speaking about my hospitalization. When I returned home, I remembered having panic attacks where I had difficulty with my breathing. It dissipated after a while, and I was thankful when things became normal again.

After this incident, I reached out to my pastor who recommended an African American therapist and psychiatrist who worked with me to develop coping skills and guidelines to manage my lifestyle, such as getting enough sleep, not overstressing and handling anger. These are important for everyone, but especially for me. They also stressed the importance of complying with the medication(s) to maintain the proper balance to continue living a normal life. I adhered to the advice of these professionals and took advantage of the time off from school and relaxed by mainly watching television. About that time, MC Hammer was one of my favorite artists to watch and I loved his song "Pump it Up" because of his energetic dance moves. Staying at home for a week was just what I needed to get my bearings back; I really needed the time off.

After two weeks of recuperating, I tried to resume my life and get caught up on my schoolwork. As the school year progressed, I managed to engage in social events with no problems. An event that I attended was my high school prom. I went with a guy I was not interested in; he was just a friend. We pretty much just went through the motions, but I longed to be at prom with the one I really loved— the one who broke my heart. He was the one I wanted to dance with when our prom theme song "Make It Last Forever" by R&B artist

Keith Sweat (from the late 1980s) played. Even though I could not "slow drag" to this love song with him, my date and I made the best of it. It was a fun night, and I would say everyone had a good time.

Despite a tumultuous year, I was proud that I graduated from high school and looked forward to college. I must say, I was pretty disappointed that my biological father did not make it to my graduation, but both of my grandmothers and parents were there. It bothered me he missed an important milestone in my life. But I also had known many disappointments before, so I should have known better and not have expected more.

Chapter 4

A Time to Plant

Merriam-Webster Dictionary states that the word plant means "to put or set in the ground for growth; to set or sow with seeds or plants; establish or institute." With all the moving around that we did in my younger years, it was definitely time for us to plant some roots and become settled. It was a while before we found a church to attend regularly. We visited a lot of them, but never really planted our roots until we joined a Lutheran church that my father's (Pete) parents had been members of for a long time. I liked the church because of the different ministries that were offered there. I was drawn to the dance ministry and was eager to become a member, so I dived in, headfirst, and became active in it before officially joining the church. I found it to be a rich experience, partly because of my dance instructor, Toni. She was an outstanding teacher who made dancing fun for all who attended her class. Looking back, she reminded me of Debbie Allen from the hit movie "Fame." She was strict and knew what she wanted from her students. She taught my god-sisters and I ballet and tap dancing. It was there that I could express myself through movement to the tune of various kinds of music. One day, the culmination of all we had learned was placed on display at a dance recital at a local school in Washington, D.C. Our costumes were amazing because she always had us adorned in vibrant, glittery colors. For this performance, she had us dressed in a gold outfit with gold fringe skirts. Everyone complimented us by letting us know how fabulous we looked! Being in these costumes always made me feel like a star. While I could always hold my own during the performances, my god-sister, Lajuan, always stole the show!

Besides dancing, I took part in drama, the choir, and I was even an acolyte. As an acolyte, my primary duties were to light the altar candles before service and to extinguish them after service and I took pleasure in doing this. At that age, it made me feel responsible. I only dabbled a little in drama, doing skits at the church from time to time. These activities made going to church fun for me. I was literally there whenever the doors opened. I loved being in the Young Inspirations youth choir because I enjoyed learning new songs, whether classical, traditional, or contemporary. I believe I was a soprano, but I was never a soloist; that was my god-sister, Sabrina. She still has a beautiful voice and sings many solos. She's so good that I ended up having her sing at my wedding. When we all sang together, we always brought the house down! We were so into it and really felt what we were singing. Her mother, my godmother, was also a talented singer, and she sang a lot in the adult choir.

Also, I took a class on catechism and after that, my mom and I were both water-baptized. According to Wikipedia, "Catechism was written by Martin Luther and published in 1529 for the training of children. Luther's small catechism reviews the Ten Commandments, the Apostles' Creed, the Lord's Prayer, The Sacrament of Holy Baptism, the Office of the Keys and Confession, and the Sacrament of the Eucharist." The class taught us about the principles of

Christianity. We were asked questions and discussed the answers in class, which I enjoyed. It allowed me to really gain a better understanding of what Lutherans believed. Furthermore, (just an FYI), in this faith, they did the sprinkling of water, not full immersion into the water for baptism.

I loved being in church because I felt exuberant, and I loved the people there. The congregants of the church were lovely people, but they were unaware of my Bipolar I. On one particular Sunday, I remembered an experience where I believed I was having an episode/crisis. I was probably manic when I felt like God was telling me to go into the church service and sing a certain song. On that Sunday, I explained to the ushers that I needed to sing my song. The church service was very regimented, with no deviation from the order; yet I wanted to disrupt the service with my song. My pastor, whom I loved dearly, allowed me to come up to him and sing it. I remembered him saying afterward that I had walked on water. I think he was preaching about Peter getting out of the boat and walking to Jesus. After my rendition, I remembered crying as I sat in the back and Pete telling me to get it together. I cried because the experience—the enormity of it all—overwhelmed me. Thankfully, no one at the church treated me unkindly. They couldn't even tell that I had an episode. I'm truly thankful that my pastor did not act out of the norm or caused me to seem like I was out of place or weird for making this request.

Matthew 14:22-34 (KJV) states, "And straightway Jesus constrained His disciples to get into a ship, and to go before Him unto the other side, while He sent the multitudes away. And when He had sent the multitudes away, He went up into a mountain apart to pray: and when the evening was come, he was there alone. But the ship was now in the midst of the sea, tossed with waves: for the wind was contrary. And in the fourth watch of the night Jesus went unto them, walking on the sea. And when the disciples saw Him walking on the sea, they were troubled, saying, It is a spirit; and they cried out for fear. But straightway Jesus spake unto them, saying, Be of good cheer; it is I; be not afraid. And Peter answered Him and said, Lord, if it be thou, bid me come unto thee on the water. And He said, Come. And when Peter was come down out of the ship, he walked on the water, to go to Jesus. But when he saw the wind boisterous, he was afraid; and beginning to sink, he cried, saying, Lord, save me. And immediately Jesus stretched forth his hand, and caught him, and said unto him, O thou of little faith, wherefore didst thou doubt? And when they were come into the ship, the wind ceased. Then they that were in the ship came and worshipped Him, saying, Of a truth thou art the Son of God."

According to Matthew Henry's commentary, this story illustrates that we have to live by faith and not by sight. In the miracle of Jesus walking on the water, "He acted as the Lord of nature… While Peter kept his eyes fixed upon Christ, and upon his word and power, he walked upon the water well enough; but when he noticed withal of the danger he was in, and observed how the floods lift up their waves, then he feared… Peter, when he saw the wind boisterous, should have remembered what he had seen (Ch. 8:27), when the winds and the sea obeyed Christ; but therefore, we fear continually every day, because we forget the Lord our Maker, (Isa. 51:12,13)."

I related this story to my singing solo experience because it was my walking on water moment. It was scary, in my state of mind, getting in front of everyone and belting out a song. I had never done or experienced anything like that before. I thank God that I had such a gracious pastor who understood my struggle. He visited my godparents' house when I was with them, and I liked him because he always talked with me and served me communion. In turn, I gave him a shell with a pearl inside a clear cube.

According to pearls.com, "natural pearls form when an irritant — usually a parasite and not the proverbial grain of sand—works its way into an oyster, mussel, or clam. As a defense mechanism, a fluid is used to coat the irritant. Layer upon layer of this coating, called 'nacre', is deposited until a lustrous pearl is formed." An unknown author puts it another way, "Did you know… An oyster that has not been wounded in any way does not produce pearls? A pearl is a healed wound. Pearls are a product of pain, the result of a foreign or unwanted substance entering the oyster, such as a parasite or a grain of sand. The inside of an oyster shell is a shiny substance called 'nacre.' When a grain of sand enters, the nacre cells go to work and cover the grain of sand with layers and more layers to protect the defenseless body from the oyster. As a result, a beautiful pearl is formed! The more pearls, the more valuable… God never allows pain without a purpose. What if your greatest ministry to others comes out of your greatest hurt? The hard things we may go through now are really nothing compared to the glory that will be revealed in us later." (Romans 8:17-18; author unknown).

Having bipolar disorder is my wound, but throughout this process, a pearl was formed—me; I was healed from this wound and today it has become my ministry. I gave my pastor a pearl in a shell that was in a glass cube for him to remember me by and thanked him for treating me like a precious pearl. Matthew 13:46 (KJV) says, "Who, when he had found one pearl of great price, went and sold all that he had, and bought it?" "The pearl is an illustration of the Church and or the Christian… The Lord is looking for something of great value and He compares it to the very best pearls. The very best pearls are the most valuable too… Just as the oyster is immersed in the ocean to accomplish the task of creating a pearl, we should be immersed in the Lord Jesus Christ to become His pearl of great price. The Church He died for and will be returning for." I thank God that Jesus valued us by paying a great price by giving His life to redeem us.

At Peace Lutheran Church, I experienced being involved in ministry and having a close relationship with the pastor, elders, teachers, and members. I definitely learned a lot spiritually and I'm glad attending this church was part of my spiritual journey. I eventually moved on as there are moments when we may outgrow situations, be it a church, school, and/or even people. When this happens, we must recognize that our assignment is over, and it's time for us to move on and grow in our spiritual walk with Christ.

As Psalms 1:3 (AMP) says, "And he will be like a tree firmly planted [and fed] by streams of water, which yield its fruit in its season; its leaf does not wither; And in whatever he does, he prospers [and comes to maturity].

Chapter 5

A Time to Pluck Up That Which is Planted

There is a time and season for everything under the sun, I felt my season had ended at my family's church, and so I moved on and joined a new church. At this new church, I felt alive, especially with the praise and worship that took place there because I had experienced nothing like it before. One of my friends invited me and immediately I knew in my spirit that this was the church for me. It was much larger than the previous churches I attended. What I enjoyed about it was how everyone was so welcoming. Even though the size of the church seemed intimidating, it was apparent that once I got involved; it did not seem so big after all. I took new members' class and then I got water baptized—full immersion this time! I took Bible classes and got involved with the evangelism ministry.

A year later, I got married at this church and started my family. But before that happy beginning with my husband, it took meeting the wrong guys to know who the right one would be. While I was in college, I realized I was somewhat promiscuous. More than I should have been based on my upbringing; I knew better. But looking back, I believe that was partly because of my manic depression or bipolar disorder, not taking my medication, and all the experiences that lead up to me being diagnosed with bipolar disorder.

I dated a guy in college who I really fell for and I spent a lot of time with him. He loved playing basketball, volleyball, and bowling. While he loved playing these sports, he had sickle cell anemia, which caused him to recover slowly whenever he had a crisis. I thought I was the only one, but I suspected he was fooling around on me with an old girlfriend. One time, I went over to his apartment and his friend would not let me in. My thought was that he more than likely had a girl in there. I was enraged when I finally got in there. Once in, I didn't see that he had a girl in there unless he hid her very well. In my anger, I pushed everything off his dresser, snatched my boom box, and left out of there.

I also dated one of the star basketball players, but that did not last long when I found out he had other groupies and girlfriends. I had other flings—I would not call them relationships—and I am so thankful I came out of them whole through all of that. Being involved in these types of situations were dangerous for me because my emotions were all over the place and it didn't help that I was not taking my medication. I would get on the road and drive aggressively and at high speeds while returning to my parents' house. My mom reminded me when we were talking one day; I don't know how I forgot this, but she and Pete took my car keys because they felt it was too dangerous for me to drive in the mental state I was in. In my anger, I called the police on them. They tried to explain why they took my keys, but their explanations did not matter to me—I just wanted my keys.

According to my mom, I had a college friend come by and pick me up from home. She reminded me that while I was in college, she and my godmother had to take me to the emergency room to get my meds because I obviously had not been taking them. My mom said she repeatedly urged me to get back on my meds before I finally agreed. My behavior was erratic, and it caused me to keep driving back and forth from home to college, which was an hour away. Apparently, I was not sleeping, and she was worried I would eventually end up getting into an accident. This occurred during my senior year of college, and my mother observed that I was very irritable and seemed stressed. I was definitely having manic episodes.

I heard a sermon by Joel Osteen that struck me because I had never heard it said that "God's grace is promiscuous. God's grace will go to anyone. Grace, He freely gives us. Freely in the original translation is promiscuous. If someone is promiscuous, they are unrestrained, they are loose." I'm glad God freely gave me grace and protected me back then. When I didn't know any better, He still watched over me and protected me from life's dangers.

When I graduated from college, I moved home for a year and then moved in with two other roommates who were also sorority sisters. I worked as an account executive with two radio stations; one was a gospel radio station. Through my dealings with churches, I met a pastor who took a liking to me. We went on a few dates and then, against my better judgement, engaged in a sexual relationship. We were never seen in public together. I knew I needed to get out of the relationship because it was wrong, and I always seemed to end up getting a urinary tract infection (UTI) with this guy. This was a sign from God to stop what I was doing. He tried to justify his actions by referring to how David (in the Bible) had sinned. But the difference between him and David was that David repented of his sins and was a man after God's own heart. He seemed only concerned about fulfilling his sexual desires. What I realized was that I definitely wanted out of the situation. I remembered praying to God and asking Him to get me out of the toxic situation I found myself in. God answered my prayer and gave me the release. From that moment, I never looked back. I vowed I would no longer engage in premarital sex and that I would wait until I got married. And waited was exactly what I did.

At the suggestion of my coworker, I went to a Honda dealership to purchase a new car because the engine had burned out of my car and I needed to replace it quickly. The general manager of the dealership helped me get a good deal and, being the salesperson that I was, I asked him about his advertising. He told me he wasn't doing anything, but he knew someone who worked in another division of the dealership who might want to do some advertising. So, I met with the manager he referred to me and he became one of my regular clients. I noticed that whenever I visited the dealership, he always did nice things for me, like wash my car and even put rims on my tires one time! I thought he liked me after his kind gestures.

We were both in relationships, but soon he ended his relationship, and I followed behind him and ended mine too. We went out and our first date was to see the movie, "Set it Off." We were supposed to meet at another time, but he stood me up. As weird as this may sound, this really got my attention and made me want to get to know him better! We had a lot in common—he was from my mom's home state of North Carolina, and we were the same age, only four months apart.

One day, we went on a date to meet my friend and her boyfriend in Philadelphia. It was not a long drive, but I drank way too much water for a road trip. I had to ask him to pull over at an overpass bridge and I hopped over the side and finally relieved myself. In the process, I snagged my stockings, and I was so embarrassed by it all. But when you have to go, you have to go! I grew to respect him because he honored my wish to wait until marriage to have sex. We got into some heavy petting though, which we later found out was wrong in our premarital counseling sessions. It was at his house during a Super Bowl party he gave me a friendship ring. I was thinking of looking for a house, but he asked me what if I married someone who already had a house. He felt there was no need for me to look for one since he already had a home. Wow, was this really happening? First the promise ring and now this! Were my dreams of being married finally coming true? Was this streak of meeting one wrong guy after another coming to an end?

On a trip to the Poconos, he called my dad, Pete, and asked him if he could marry me and Pete said yes! Then I said yes! Finally, the day came; I was engaged to be married! That was one of the best days of my life. I couldn't stop smiling, grinning from ear-to-ear. Every girl waits in anticipation of this day, and it finally happened for me. I had found my helpmate, and all was right in my world.

A funny incident that happened on the trip was trying to teach him how to ski. While we were on the ski lift, I told him to prepare to get off. He thought I said get off right then, and he jumped off into a small ditch! It shocked me he did that, but I could do nothing for him and continued on the ski lift until it was time to get off. Once I got off, I frantically went to find him to make sure he was ok. Thankfully, he was not hurt but maybe his pride was a little. Needless to say, he has not tried to ski since, and I never tried again to teach him!

After accepting his proposal, we started the marital process and took part in premarital counseling, which lasted for nine months. It was pretty intense and taught us things about ourselves and each other that we did not know. We pressed through and completed the process. Doing the premarital counseling was good for us because it allowed us to give serious thought to the seriousness of marriage and what we were entering. Often, we fantasize about being married, but it's not a fairytale like we see in the movies and should not be entered into lightly. It requires work, work, work, and commitment. After completing this process, he joined my church, attended the new members' class and got water baptized. I loved how committed he was. We were becoming unified partners in life and still are today.

My husband and I married on October 25, 1997 and had a beautiful wedding at our church. I wanted my family and friends in attendance and those who participated in our wedding to feel moved by the ceremony. Before I walked down the aisle, I had dancers called "Spirit Wings" to perform a dance to Richard Smallwood's song, "Thank you" and I had the Voices of Heaven 600 choir to sing, "Total Praise" also by Richard Smallwood. One highlight of the ceremony was when my husband-to-be gave me a three-point kiss; first on the forehead, then on the cheek, and then on the lips. The audience went wild! Everything was beautiful, with everyone having a good time. The reception was a blur; we were so busy greeting people that we hardly ate! Thank goodness we thought ahead and packed doggy bags!

We stayed the night at the Doubletree hotel at BWI Airport where we were greeted by their signature warm chocolate chip cookies and then left out for our honeymoon in Jamaica! We had a wonderful time in Ocho Rios and Montego Bay and, of course, the famous Dunn's River Falls. I tried my hand at water skiing like I'd done in the hay days of my youth, while my husband watched helplessly on the beach. For the life of me, I could not get up on those skis. My husband begged me to give it up and come back to the shore where he was, and so I did.

One thing we enjoyed about our time in Jamaica was the food. The authentic, well-seasoned food such as curry and jerk chicken, oxtail with rice and peas, plantains, beef patties and coco bread are delicious foods the island is known for. We definitely enjoyed the scrumptious meals we ate daily. My husband's favorite meal was the jerk chicken. The whole time we were there, he mainly ate jerk chicken and fries. No matter where we went to eat, that was what his palate had a taste for. With jerk chicken being one of the popular dishes in Jamaica, what better place to get it!

Not long after we got married, I became pregnant with our first child and the honeymoon was over. I remembered I was on a business trip to Minneapolis and somehow mixed up my birth control pills. I think that may have contributed to me getting pregnant unexpectedly. This was not what we had planned so soon, but it turned out to be a wonderful blessing with the birth of our son.

I remembered being in labor on my birthday on 9-11. As a birthday treat and to get my mind off the fact that I was in labor, my husband and I went to the movie theater to see the movie, "Why Do Fools Fall in Love." It was a pretty wonderful movie that we both enjoyed, but the labor pains seemed to have lasted all night. Not too long after my husband left for work, the pains became so intense that I got my brother-in-law to help me. Thank God he was living with us or I don't know what I would have done. He came to my rescue and ended up taking me to the hospital, as I could no longer deal with the excruciating pain I was in. Not too long after showing up at the hospital, the doctors sent me back home because I guess they thought the labor pains or dilation was not significant enough for them to admit me yet. I was home not long before a friend called me to see how I was doing, but I could barely talk—I was in so much pain. She asked for my husband's number to inform him he had to take me to the hospital. I told my parents, who were on their way to take me out to dinner, to meet us at the hospital instead. When my husband arrived at our home, he frantically gathered my already packed baby/delivery bag and quickly, but carefully, drove us to the hospital.

Once I was in the care of the doctors and nurses, my husband stepped away to go back to the car to get my belongings. I think the reality of it all was sinking in for him because it took him a long time to get back—becoming a father was really hitting him. Thankfully, my mother showed up and was right by my side. She reassured and comforted me while my husband was away. She held my hand, and I could have broken all of her fingers because I squeezed her hand for dear life because the pain was so intense. I felt so much pressure and wanted this ordeal to be over. My husband finally came back, and they told him to get ready to go with me for surgery because I was going to have a C-section. With this being his first child, my husband was nervous, and it was all over him. He told my mom she could go in with me, but she insisted he should go instead since he was my husband and soon to be a father. She felt this was a life-changing experience that he should and needed to be a part of—scared or not.

On September 12, 1998, my firstborn (and only) son was born! My husband was ecstatic that he was now a first-time father. A mild-mannered man who doesn't display emotions much, the nervousness that engulfed him was replaced with thoughts of ownership of his son he helped to bring into the world. He was now a proud papa, on cloud nine with a blue cigar and all. While it excited me that my baby was born, I was so worn out from the experience that I don't remember if my husband actually cut the umbilical cord or kissed me on my forehead after he saw his son for the first time.

All my friends and family visited me while I was in the hospital. It was great to see everyone because they were all so eager to see my baby. With all the excitement, my doctor and the nurses had to prepare me to go home because I did not need to stay in the hospital beyond the time allocated for C-sections. For the most part, I was in good health, but before I could go home, I had to walk around the ward and pass some of the air from my stomach. After doing this repeatedly, I was ready to go home. When I was released from the hospital and we arrived home, my husband was extra careful with the precious cargo (his son and I) that he was now responsible for. He slowly walked me to our front door with our baby snuggled in his baby seat. When we settled in, it was like we were in awe as we stared at the beautiful and perfect baby we had created.

Everyone was elated for us. My parents were engrossed with their first grandchild. He especially brought so much joy to my mom. She loved how he flipped his skinny legs from side to side while at the hospital. I thanked God for my mom because she helped me out tremendously my first few days of being home. My husband did not take any time off from work and after a while, I was left alone with our baby. I was breastfeeding and doing well. My friends thought I was so anal for recording the times when I breastfed and from which breast. I wrote it down to keep track because I did not want to get engorged! It was very painful whenever this happened; therefore, I made it a point to avoid this from happening.

The job I had at the time let me work from home for the entire 12 weeks, and I was grateful for that. Taking care of an infant by myself was no easy feat. Sometimes I felt overwhelmed and drained; I could not wait for my husband to get home to give me a break. I felt trapped because I was the only one who could feed our baby in the beginning until I started breast pumping. This was because the doctors didn't want the baby to have nipple confusion, so they encouraged me to wait to introduce the bottle. When it was time to have him on the bottle, I could not wait! This meant I could catch a break and have my husband feed him from time to time; I really needed the break.

As we became adjusted to being newlyweds and new parents, at some point, I started having delusions of grandeur. While in church one day, I was thinking about my husband being up there with the Apostles of God and that I needed to give a large donation to the church. So, I wrote a check in the amount of $4500—we could not afford this, but for some reason, I felt we could. My husband got wind of this and intercepted it. I was having an episode/crisis and didn't realize it.

In another instance, while in church one particular Sunday, I went to the bathroom and took off all of my son's clothing, even his diaper. What I was going to do with him naked, I do not know—sacrifice him, maybe? One of my friends, who was a member of the church, came into the bathroom and saw what I had done and asked that someone get my husband. The next thing I remembered were the ushers putting me in a wheelchair and rolling me out to the car. My husband drove me and my son to my parents' home because we always went there after church. When we arrived there, I must have continued to do or say something out of character. At some point, I called my father the anti-Christ and the next thing I knew, my mom was taking me to the hospital; however, she did not want me to go to the hospital that I had gone to when I was 17. She knew the hospitals better in that area where they lived than my husband did. When she checked me into this particular hospital, I remembered wanting to get out of the ER even if I was only wearing one of those hospital gowns with my butt hanging out. It was like the Jack Nicholson scene in the movie, "Something Has Gotta Give." My poor mom kept trying to rein me in. They transported me to a hospital in Montgomery County (Md), and I remembered the pain I was in because my milk was drying up and I could not breastfeed my baby anymore. Also, I remembered taking off all my clothes and walking out into the hallway from my room. Clearly, I was experiencing mental episodes that caused me to do some pretty outlandish things. But God had an angel in the hospital walls to assist me. Someone from my church worked there, and I remembered him being so gracious and kind. I don't remember the details of how he helped me, but just his presence and knowing that someone I could relate to was there, was reassuring to me. I recalled my husband visiting with our son and I was so happy to see them and was even more grateful that his grandmother took care of our baby while I was hospitalized. I was on maternity leave from my job and working from home, so this episode did not affect my work. After a week of being hospitalized, they finally released me. But I sure wish someone would have told me that having a baby along with postpartum depression was a mixture that would kick me into an episode with my bipolar disorder!

According to the American Psychiatric Association, peripartum depression (formerly known as postpartum depression) "refers to depression occurring during pregnancy or after childbirth. An estimated one in seven women experiences peripartum depression." What I believe I experienced was peripartum psychosis. The American Psychiatric Association also states, "Peripartum psychosis is an extremely rare but serious condition that occurs in only one or two out of every 1,000 deliveries. The symptoms of peripartum psychosis are extreme and may include insomnia, excessive energy, agitation, hearing voices, and extreme paranoia or suspiciousness. Many women with peripartum psychosis have a personal or family history of bipolar disorder. Symptoms of peripartum psychosis can be a serious medical emergency and require immediate attention." To hammer this home even further, Postpartum.net states, "In her psychotic state, the delusions and beliefs make sense to her. They feel very real to her and are often religious." I think this best summarized how I felt during that time.

My mom informed me that the nurse said I was able to rebound and do well because I had so much family support. Ten years had passed since I had my first episode in high school and had to be hospitalized at 17 years old. Having the second hospitalization at 27, I recognized God sustained me and kept me in my right mind. 1 Peter 5:8 (KJV) states, "Be sober, be vigilant; because your adversary the devil, as a roaring lion, walketh about, seeking whom he may devour." The devil was trying to steal, kill, and destroy me. He tried to use a joyful event in my life to take me out! But what the enemy meant for evil, God worked it out for my good.

Chapter 6

A Time to Heal

The word *heal* means "to make sound or whole again; to restore back to health," according to Webster's Dictionary. And the truth is, we all need to heal from something in our lives. After my last episode stemming from stripping my son nude in church and having to be hospitalized, things went back to normal once I was released. I picked up where my life left off and continued with life as usual. However, what I should have done was take some time to ponder on what I had done with my son. I needed to spend some time to myself and do some introspection and heal from the guilt I felt because things could have gone in a different direction.

When I reunited with my baby, I held him close and kissed his little face, thankful he was okay by the grace of God. In time, I learned to forgive myself, understanding that I have a medical condition that triggers me from time to time if I don't take proper care of myself by taking my meds. Initially, I prayed to God to help me deal with it the best I could, because I condemned myself and felt guilty for my actions.

Guilt can raise its ugly head and cause us to replay events over and over in our minds, resulting in us condemning ourselves. In situations like these, we must know that we can turn to God and ask for forgiveness, because He is a gracious and forgiving God. We have to seek Him because He is the ultimate mind-regulator. Romans 8:1 (AMP) says, "Therefore there is now no condemnation [no guilty verdict, no punishment] for those who are in Christ Jesus [who believe in Him as personal Lord and Savior]."

While we need to learn how to forgive ourselves, we must also learn how to forgive others. Forgiving others is not always easy to do. As humans, when we are hurt by someone, it's difficult to forgive; but somehow, we must find a way to forgive that person for inflicting pain on us. When someone hurts or betrays us, our natural inclination is to want to hurt them back. However, when we can get to a place where we no longer replay or rehearse events in our minds, when we can encounter that person and no longer feel anger, rage or the hurt they caused us, then we are on the road to true forgiveness. In the grand scheme of things, walking around with unforgiveness in our hearts is not the will of God and certainly not good for our overall well-being. It can tamper with our minds as well, causing us to do dangerous things to ourselves or others. Therefore, we must grasp hold of our thoughts. 2 Corinthians 10: 3-5 (KJV) comes to mind as I speak about gaining control of our thoughts. It states, "For though we walk in the flesh, we do not war after the flesh: (For the weapons of our warfare are not carnal, but mighty through God to the pulling down of strongholds;) Casting down imaginations, and every high thing that exalteth itself against the knowledge of God, and bringing into captivity every thought to the obedience of Christ..."

I was distraught after the event with my son and being hospitalized, but I am glad to know that God can meet us where we are, even when we are at the end of our lives or feel like it is the end of life. There is always hope when we look to Jesus. He is our hope, and He can heal and restore us, making us new creatures in Him.

As we are speaking about healing, I'm currently in the healing process myself, as I recognize I have to come to terms with exercising forgiveness with my biological father. It's difficult for me to discuss my relationship with him, but as I write my thoughts down on paper, I realize this is part of my healing process. As I mentioned previously, my father and I have had a relationship from afar, but I have always hoped one day we could repair and improve it and be closer.

Since my father served in the military, there were times in my younger years when he could not be around for important events in my life because duty called. For starters, he was not present when my mother gave birth to me because he was on active duty (no fault of his own) and met me as a newborn baby when he was able to return home. Even though he was in the military, I didn't realize he would not play an active role in my life as my father. While I'm grateful to Pete for stepping up and being the father that I needed him to be, I still longed to share a closer bond with my biological father.

Unfortunately, over the course of my life, this longing was never fulfilled. I had to come to terms with the fact that my biological father would not be who I wanted him to be in my life. Even though I craved a relationship with him, I recognized that he simply was not going to be there for me or my important life events. He did not attend my high school and college graduations, and I worked hard to graduate from high school despite the setback I had with the breakdown earlier in that year. I duly noted his absence. For each graduation, I wanted my father's acceptance and validation; I wanted him to recognize and be proud of my accomplishments; after all, it was not always easy for me, and I just wanted him to be supportive of my journey.

When I was planning my wedding, I decided to have Pete walk me down the aisle. I informed my biological father I felt this honor should have been bestowed on Pete because he was always there for me as a father. To have it any other way would have been an insult to Pete since he stepped up and took on the role of father in my life. Of course, my biological father was angered by this and decided not to come to my wedding. But I felt he should have understood, given the fickle nature of our relationship. Because of his absence in our lives, he missed out on a lot. He was unable to form a relationship with my husband, children, and grandchildren. I am saddened that he doesn't know this part of his family. If he only knew how wonderful they are—his heart would melt. I hoped as my family grew with his grandchildren and great-grandchildren, they would have been the catalyst for him to get to know his family better, but that was not the case. I hoped he would've had a change of heart.

There is a level of abandonment (rejection) that is felt when a parent is not or chooses not to be a part of a child's life. The limited interaction between my biological father and me caused me to feel a void. Feelings of being unwanted and unloved became commonplace as I wondered why my father did not want to play a role in my life. Every child needs the love and affections of their parents, whether they are separated/divorced or not. Even though I have a father-figure in Pete, I still wanted my biological father in my life as well. I wish our communication was more in person than limited to texts and phone conversations.

Even though this was the situation we were in, something wonderful still came out of it—I found solace in meeting my sister! She lived in Texas with her mother, and we finally met when she was about 11 and my son was about to turn one-year-old. I'm glad I reached out to her, and that we made the connection because now we have a bond. It's good to have someone who understands and for that, I'm extremely thankful to her. In meeting with her, we realized we share similar experiences with our father. She also does not have a close relationship with him.

Even though my biological father and I are not as close as I wanted us to be, through it all, I continue to reach out and keep some sort of connection with him. Sending pictures of my children and grandchildren was a way in which I tried to stay connected. I tried another way when I invited him (before he moved to another state) to see the last Star Wars movie in the saga. I really hoped he would have agreed to this because it would have meant a lot to me because he took me to see the first Star Wars movie when I was young. Seeing the last one with him would have been a special moment for me because it was not just another movie; it would have been quality time spent with my father.

As we all know, Star Wars was epic! It was so impactful that some of the actors expressed their views on the movie. In the documentary, Obi Wan Kenobi A Jedi's Return, O'Shea Jackson Jr., who played Roken said, "Star Wars was a huge, huge part of my life. Many people like me grew up on this saga. They saw it with family, so it had a connection to family." Ewan McGregor who played Obi Wan said, "I don't think there is anything like Star Wars. It's just everywhere… it's global, it's international, it is all over the world." Hayden Christensen who played Darth Vader said, "Star Wars has this staying power. I think that's because we are able to learn about ourselves and the world around us through them. We learn about good and evil and what it is to be a hero. Giving yourself to something bigger than you." The director of Obi Wan Kenobi series Deborah Chow also said, "It's in everybody's life. Everybody's grown up with it in some respect… So many people have such an emotional relationship to it and so it is quite meaningful in the broader context of your life." This all explains why I really wanted to watch the final episode of this classic movie with my father, but sadly, we were unable to make it happen.

It seemed that all my efforts to connect with my biological father failed. Despite this, I never lost my desire to maintain some form of communication with him. I will continue trying because in my heart, I want our relationship to be more than what it is currently. Even though he was not present during my formative years through adulthood, I still desire to have a connection with him. As I pondered on why my father's presence was so sorely missed, I realized it was because one of my primary love languages is quality time.

According to Gary Chapman's popular book, "The Five Love Languages: How to Express Heartfelt Commitment to Your Mate,' 'A central aspect of quality time is togetherness." This does not just apply to your mate; it can apply to all of your relationships. Chapman continues to say, "The important thing emotionally is that we are spending focused time with each other. The activity is the vehicle that creates the sense of togetherness. The important thing about the father rolling the ball to the two-year-old is not the activity itself, but the emotions that are created between the father and his child… What happens on the emotional level is what matters. Our spending time together in a common pursuit communicates that we care about each other, that we like to do things together." Chapman could not have said this any better; he hit the nail on the head. Spending time with my biological father was what I craved. While I love Star Wars, what would have mattered most to me would have been the quality time spent with him. For every girl craves the attention of her father and that's what the young girl in me desired.

I would have taken any type of in-person interaction with my biological father. I especially wanted him to be around when I had my first breakdown. I wish he would have been there more to check up on how I was doing after his visit to the hospital. I also longed for quality conversations that went beyond a text message or brief phone conversation. Chapman says, "Quality conversation requires not only sympathetic listening but also self-revelation." I wanted to get to know my dad so that he could reveal more of himself to me. It is hard to feel close to someone who you don't feel you know. If he were present in my life, I would not have felt the constant sense of being abandoned and my choices in men in my younger years may have been different. I think his absence in my life caused me to accept less than what I deserved.

Through it all, I learned to stop putting my expectation in him, my earthly father, and put my expectation in God. But most importantly, I decided to not let this define me and who I am. I discovered I had to stop feeling like the victim and realized that I was a victor; I am a victor! I heard someone say there is victory in my vulnerability. And this is the reason why I am sharing this part of my life that needs healing. Hebrews 13:5 (KJV) says, "I will never leave thee nor forsake thee." This is comforting to know that whether my biological father is present in my life or not, I know God will always be there for me. Matthew 28:20 (KJV) says, "I am with you always, even unto the end of the world." When I think about it, I am blessed to have two fathers; some people don't even have one. My father, Pete, stood in the gap when my biological father was not there, and I am grateful for that. He loves me as if I were his own, and that within itself is a true blessing.

According to Afro.com, "38.7% of African American children under 18 live with both parents. Instead, more than one-third of all Black children in the United States under the age of 18 live with unmarried mothers." I thank God that I grew up in a two-parent home.

Although I do not have the relationship that I've always wanted with my biological father (yet), I still hold on to hope that we will get there, eventually. I pray that this day will come. His absence and lack of affirmation (I feel) contributed to my having low self-esteem and a sense of unworthiness. However, a light bulb went off when the First Lady of my former church quoted Psalm 139:14 (KJV) to me. It states, "I am fearfully and wonderfully made." When she told me this, it was a revelation to me because I had never heard that Scripture before or if I had, it was the first time I viewed it as pertaining to me. It confirmed for me I was wonderfully made by God, and today I accept this truth as my reality. Despite not having my biological father in my life, I've learned to accept the things I cannot change concerning my father and to take life one day at a time. As my therapist said, situations will resurface regarding him, but I have to close them each time, manage my expectations and keep on managing them. I have to protect my mental health.

The world would say I have reason to give up on my father, but God says in Romans 12:2 (KJV), "And be not conformed to this world: but be ye transformed by the renewing of your mind." So, I have decided that I am going to remain open and continue to love my father because no matter the difficulties, I know he loves me. I believe God can redeem the time and, according to Joel 2:25 (KJV), God "will restore to you (me) the years that the locust hath eaten." Through the first Adam, Romans 3:23 (KJV) states, "For all have sinned, and come short of the glory of God." Through the second Adam—Jesus Christ— atonement is offered to all." So, I choose life and I choose to be better, not bitter.

I have seen the goodness of God time and time again in my life and I know He is healing me day by day, changing me from glory to glory. I realized the need to forgive my father for my healing when I truly understood that prayers are hindered when I hold on to unforgiveness. I also recognized that if I don't forgive, God won't forgive me. I still hold on to the hope that one day my biological father and I will get there. Anything is possible.

49

Chapter 7

A Time to Break Down & A Time to Build Up

I was looking at what it means to "break down" in the Bible and it never occurred to me that the story of Job, which we heard and quoted Scripture so much is the perfect example of how we are to be when we feel broken down. The book of Job asks, "Why does the righteous suffer?" It says in the Amplified Bible (Job 1:3), that Job "was an extremely rich man who was also God-fearing." It also says in Job 1:8-12 (AMP), "And the Lord said to Satan, "Have you considered My servant Job, that there is none like him on the earth, a blameless and upright man, one who [reverently] fears God and abstains from and shuns evil [because it is wrong]?" Then Satan answered the Lord, "Does Job [reverently] fear God for nothing? Have You not put a hedge about him and his house and all that he has, on every side? You have conferred prosperity and happiness upon him in the work of his hands, and his possessions have increased in the land. But put forth Your hand now and touch all that he has, and he will curse You to Your face. And the Lord said to Satan [the adversary and the accuser], Behold, all that he has is in your power, only upon the man himself put not forth your hand. So, Satan went forth from the presence of the Lord."

Some of us are familiar with the story of Job and how he was stripped of everything he held dear, but he did not lose his faith or become bitter. Job said in the heavily quoted Scripture, Job 13:15 (KJV), "Though he slay me, yet will I trust in Him." God never said this life would be easy. He said to deny ourselves, pick up our cross daily and follow Him. He also said it rains on the just and the unjust. I mention Job not because my struggles compare to his, but because we question why God allows certain things to happen in our lives or why we struggle with certain things God permits. Ephesians 6:12 (KJV) states, "For we wrestle not against flesh and blood, but against principalities, against powers, against rulers of the darkness of this world, against spiritual wickedness in high places." The Apostle Paul asked God to remove the thorn from his flesh. God did not remove the thorn so that he would not boast but remain humble. Paul learned that God's power is made perfect in our weakness.

God tells us in 2 Corinthians 10:4 (AMP), "For the weapons of our warfare are not physical [weapons of flesh and blood], but they are mighty before God for the overthrow and destruction of strongholds. [Insomuch as we] refute arguments and theories and reasonings and every proud and lofty thing that sets itself up against the [true] knowledge of God; and we lead every thought and purpose away captive into the obedience of Christ [the Messiah, the Anointed One]." According to Great Bible study, "Strongholds are merely incorrect thinking patterns." We can break them down with the Sword of the Spirit, which is the Word of God (Bible), our spiritual weapon.

We have to be mindful of the strongholds in our lives, especially if we wrestle with bipolar or any other mental disorder. While being a bridesmaid at a girlfriend's wedding, I thought I might be pregnant with my second child. I did not have any symptoms really, but maybe a missed menstrual cycle. It was just a feeling I had, and I found out I definitely was when I went to see the doctor. I'm thankful I did not have hard pregnancies with my son or daughter. However, I did struggle mentally. I was not taking my medication at the time and the further I went along in my pregnancy, the more things spiraled out of control again. I was very agitated and with everything I said, my reactions were exaggerated and way out of proportion to what was happening, per my mom. So, on a scale from 1 to 10, my behavior was a 10 and there was no reasoning with me. My husband said I was not sleeping and because of my manic behavior, my mom and husband reached out to a psychiatrist to get me back on medications to help me.

During my pregnancy, my hormones were already raging, but add to that having a mental disorder or a chemical imbalance, and the experience (again) became extremely overwhelming for me to bear. I had to find a way to become balanced again. Because of the episode with my son where I stripped him down naked in church, my husband and mother were very concerned. They did not want a repeat of what happened back then, nor did I. Reluctantly, I got back on my medication to avoid having another hospitalization.

To help me deal with my disorder while I was pregnant, my psychiatrist found a medication I could take that would not harm the baby. This was a good fit for both of us, and I have been on this same medication ever since—I have not had another hospitalization either. I'm so thankful for the love and support my mother and husband showed me. They were beneficial in keeping me on the straight and narrow. Nahum 1:9 (KJV) says, "affliction shall not rise up the second time." I'm glad the affliction did not rise up again for me. God is a good God, and He will always place the right people in our lives just when we need support and encouragement.

After the birth of my daughter, I had to meditate on the Word. In Psalm 1:3 (KJV) it says, "And he shall be like a tree planted by the rivers of water, that bringeth forth his fruit in his season; his leaf also shall not wither; and whatsoever he doeth shall prosper." We need people in our lives to keep us balanced and on stable ground. As I said before, God, my husband, and mother kept me grounded. Now I have to pass on what I have learned to help my children stay rooted and grounded as well.

And with so many things going on in the world—rising gas prices, inflation, recession, political division, wars and rumors of wars, we most definitely have to be grounded and find a way to gird up our minds during these hard economic times. 1 Peter1:13 (KJV) says, "Wherefore gird up the loins of your mind, be sober, and hope to the end for the grace that is to be brought unto you at the revelation of Jesus Christ." With what seem like mayhem taking place across the world, some would say we are living in perilous times; the world is coming to an end soon; prophesy is being fulfilled with the wars that are going on right now in the Middle East and Ukraine. Witnessing different events taking place on the news can really cause us to experience anxiety; therefore, we must find ways to safeguard our mental well-being as this is very important.

People may feel that mental illness refers to those who wrestle with depression, schizophrenia, or like me, battle with bipolar disorder. The truth is, we all deal with mental health issues each time we feel anxiety, sadness, and/or depression. What do we do when we have these emotions? How do we cope with them? Do we have an outlet to express our genuine emotions? Whether it's a therapist, friend or family member, it's important to speak to someone about the emotions we feel. It helps to speak with someone, so please don't feel ashamed or fearful to reach out to someone like a therapist. It's so important to communicate. Oftentimes, life can throw us some heavy blows, so we have to be there for each other. Therefore, it's important to gird up our minds to equip ourselves from the various thoughts that can cloud our minds from life events.

The movie, "Overcomer," is an example of someone who had to gird up her mind. An asthmatic African American girl, named Hannah, is the school's only cross-country runner. Coming from a broken home without a mother or father, she was raised by her grandmother. With no mother, and her father presumed dead, she was a loner who was also a thief, but she was destined to be a great cross-country runner even though it seemed unlikely at the time. Although she was the only member on the team, her coach trained her anyway. One day, he ended up in the hospital and accidentally entered a room and befriended a gentleman, who unbeknownst to him happened to be this young lady's father. He connected her to her father, who became another coach to her while he was hospitalized. During his hospitalization, she secretly visited her father (without her grandmother's knowledge) and they reconnected and forged a relationship.

As a former runner back in his heyday, he stepped in like an assistant coach from his hospital bed and trained his daughter to become a better cross-country runner. The original coach was a basketball coach and because of funding constraints, ended up becoming the cross-country coach that year. Long story short, the father-daughter duo bonded. He coached her remotely where he strategically showed her how to win races. Hannah was given ear buds and a player and was told to play the player at the beginning of the race. She was pleasantly surprised to learn it was her dad she heard speaking to her as she ran this championship race. He gave her encouraging instructions along the way. And who wouldn't be motivated to keep pressing forward in the race after hearing, "This is your dad. I'm going to coach you through this race and be with you every step of the way." In the end, she ended up winning the championship. Her father passed away and even in death, he still encouraged her. As a father who received another opportunity to develop a relationship with his long-lost daughter, he created other recordings that she could listen to during momentous times in her life, such as milestone birthdays and graduations, for example. He knew he would not be with her always and as a caring father, made sure he continued to encourage her while she ran her races in college and in life.

The reason for sharing this story is to show the importance of having someone on your side to keep you grounded and focused. How fortunate was she to have a father to listen to, who encouraged her? Hannah gave her all in the race and kept her focus on her father's instructions. This made her mentally sound to push forward in order to win the race, despite her shortcomings. Though she was a loner who had asthma and self-doubt she eventually learned how to gird up her mind in order to run and win races.

I could relate to this movie because God, my heavenly Father, continues to coach me through life. Despite my own shortcomings with having Bipolar I, He encourages and validates me by letting me know who I am in Him. What I know for certain is that He will always be there for me, guiding me through this thing called life.

As we run our personal races in life, we ought to be like Hannah and learn to depend on our heavenly father, Jesus Christ, to give us instructions on how to win our own races. We must gird up our minds, putting aside self-doubt, low self-esteem, and any negative thoughts that may plague our minds. I'm reminded of a sermon my pastor preached, "Run Your Race," where he stated, "We are not spectators, we are competitors in this race… we are not supposed to look outside our lanes. God has a course, path, purpose for us to run with patience. Run to win at every age. Get back in the race and run because God only gives us one life." This sermon really resonated with me because we have to be focused and vigilant in life. Daily, we face many challenges that serve as distractions that can take us off course if we are not careful. After overcoming many obstacles in my life, I've learned to stay in my lane and keep moving, girding up my mind as I go along.

I'd like to reiterate that girding up the mind speaks to controlling the many thoughts that run through our heads constantly. As we go throughout our day, we wrestle with many voices—some good; some bad. There are many negative and positive thoughts that can affect the way our days will go. If we are not careful, the negative ones can really tear us down mentally. In Rick Renner's Sparkling Gems from the Greek, he says, "gird up the loins comes from the Greek word anadzonnumi. This word was used to describe Orientals who wore long robes. Before taking a long journey or before running a race, they would gather up their loose robes and tuck them under their girdle." This is a metaphor for the mind. We must constantly renew our minds from wrong thinking that will hinder our progress in finishing the race and walking with God. Rick Renner goes on to say, "that Peter is not talking about a garment made of material; he is referring to the loins of our minds." Rick Renner goes on to say, "You see Peter is telling us that if we don't:

- Deal with the loose ends that exist in our minds and emotions;

- Correct those parts of our thinking that we know are wrong;

- Grab hold of all those dangling areas in our thinking and put them out of the way;

- And remove them by the authority of the Word of God;

- Then we are choosing to permit things to exist in our lives that will hinder our steps and slow us down in our race and in our ability to successfully walk with God!"

In the movie, "The Devil Wears Prada" I love when the character, Nigel (played by Stanley Tucci) said, "Alright everyone, gird your loins!" when Meryl Streep's character, Miranda, arrived at the office earlier than expected and everyone frantically scurried to get ready for her entrance. He was telling them to prepare for action in that critical moment. Because Miranda was a very intimidating and difficult personality—no one knew what her behavior was going to be like, they had to prepare for any negative speech she was going to throw their way. Was she going to say something derogatory? Was she going to put someone down because they displeased her with something they had done? Or was she going to say something kind? Since she was so erratic in her behavior, people walked around on eggshells. A personality like hers can bring about great stress for anyone who has to interact with it. Not only that, for the individuals being demeaned or talked down to, it can affect that person's self-esteem. So, in real life, when we encounter personalities like these, we have to not allow their negativity to affect our emotions. We must recognize the problem is with the negative personality, not you. Therefore, know or learn how to gird up your mind against negativity and negative people.

While writing this book, I heard an evangelist say, "You have to tuck under your belt to not be hindered, distracted or your mobility will be affected. She mentioned that you have to bind strongholds or negative thoughts that keep you from moving free or forward. Also, she said gird up the truth of God's Word and capture thoughts, anything that would impede, cripple, stop, or get you off course. She said we don't have time to sit on our loins, but be sober, be alert and meditate on the Word of God. We are to roll up our sleeves, be prepared, tuck ourselves in the Word of truth (Bible), and to guard our hearts and minds because the devil will not stop attacking our minds. She said we have to work at it and fight the good fight of faith."

To summarize things, in one of Joel Osteen's sermons, "Fight for Your Future," he preached on how the devil does not fight you where you are, he fights you for where you are going, and it does not have to be fair. He attacks you because he knows what is in you. He knows you are a giant killer and history maker. So, protect your mind. Take care of your mental health— gird it up!

For professional help with your mental health, here are some excellent resources:

1. NAMI-National Alliance on Mental Illnes-1-800-950-NAMI (6264) M-F 10 a.m.-10 p.m. EST
2. BMHA-The Black Mental Health Alliance 410-338-2642
3. National Suicide Prevention Line 1-800-273-TALK (8255)
4. SAMHSA-Substance Abuse and Mental Health Services Administration-1-800-662-HELP (4357)
5. Suicide & Crisis Lifeline Call 9-8-8- or text HOME to 741741 for Free, 24/7, for confidential crisis counseling

Chapter 8

A Time to Weep

Dictionary.com says to weep is "to express grief, sorrow or any overpowering emotion by shedding tears." This emotion is not one that most of us want to experience, yet we will experience it at some point in our lives. Fortunately for me, I must say, I have been blessed because I have not experienced a disproportionate amount of grief during my lifetime. However, I have shed a lot of tears. An instance that caused me to lament over one of my children was when I became a grandparent unexpectedly because my son became a teenaged father. I could not believe the news.

Every parent wants their child to realize their dreams, so this new reality was huge. Of course, I grieved the loss of innocence for him in his youth and the trauma it brought to all of us. In the end, it turned out to be a welcomed blessing. Initially, I grappled with the immense hurt and tears but had to once again, gird up my mind. I had to think about the welfare of my child, the mother of the baby, and this new baby that was on the way—our world changed in an instant.

While this was a difficult pill to swallow for both families, my son and the mother of his child graduated from college, and he became

61

an independent young adult; one that I am proud of. Today, we love our granddaughter. Even though this was my son's circumstance, it was an extremely stressful time for me. I was thankful because God carried me through this period without a major episode! To help me deal with the reality of the situation, I leaned on the verse from Psalm 30:5 (KJV), where it states, "Weeping may endure for a night, but joy cometh in the morning." I experienced feeling depressed sometimes but didn't remain in that state for too long as I took comfort in the thought that God puts my tears into a bottle and that Jesus understands our pain and infirmities because even He wept!

Experiencing grief is a tough emotion to feel. We feel it after we've lost a loved one, a relationship, a job or a furry family member. I have not experienced death as much in my lifetime as some; however, death, as we all know, affects everyone. For me, the first loss was the death of my sweet aunt, my paternal grandmother's sister. She helped to raise my biological father, and I visited her often. I recalled how she took care of me when I was sick with chickenpox and how she used to let me eat coffee ice cream. When she and my uncle died, she left her house to my dad and I. She had a beautiful home that had land enough to grow crops in the backyard. It was because of her generosity and the scholarships I received I was able to attend college debt free! She showed benevolence and blessed us immensely with this gesture upon her death.

Following her death was my grandmother, who always paid special attention to me when I visited her in Virginia during the summer. It seemed like she stopped at every store on route 301 on our way to her house from Maryland. "Peebles" was one of her favorite department stores to shop at as we traveled. This was a discount store that carried an assortment of items at a reasonable cost. She always let me pick out my favorite cereal and let me eat as much as I wanted. I think my cousins sometimes were jealous of the attention she showered on me. She spoiled me and did not allow me to do as many chores like hanging the clothes on the line. Since she lived in the country, she did not have a bathroom in the house, but an outhouse instead. At night, we had to use a bedpan if we had to go to the bathroom. That took some getting used to and certainly made me appreciate the bathroom we had in the house once I returned home. I also remembered the mosquitos tearing me up! I don't think anyone else was bitten quite as much as I was. It was so bad I was even bitten once on my eyelid!

The summer months were relaxing and filled with fun as a child. Living in the country with my cousins, one thing I enjoyed doing with them was going roller skating. I wasn't a professional skater, but I could keep up with minimal falls and I eventually got it down pat. I also loved when my aunt pressed or straightened my hair with the hot comb. Sitting next to the stove with the hot comb laying on the stove and then hearing the sizzling sound as the heat hit my hair, which was laced with hair grease, is a sound I will always remember. Feeling the heat from the hot comb against my skin made me nervous because it always felt like it was going to burn my skin. When it was all over, my hair was beautiful; nice and straight and I always felt so pretty afterward. That was country living, and I often took in the fresh air and cool breeze that it brought on a hot summer's day. These were great childhood memories that I will always cherish. Just spending time with my father's side of the family gave me a connection I did not have with him. I liked the fact that everyone was so welcoming, not just my family but the people in the community as well.

There was only one memory I wish I could forget, something that my grandmother did that stuck with me for years and that did little for my self-esteem. She always called me ugly as a term of endearment.

It was her way of teasing me; I guess you would say, but deep down, I always felt uncomfortable with her calling me that name. Writing this book allowed me to peel back the layers a bit and really discover some deep-rooted issues from within and where they stemmed from. I realized how repeatedly hearing the word "ugly" deeply cut to my soul, however "unintentional" my grandmother may have meant it. Subconsciously, I believe this negatively affected my self-esteem.

Whether or not it was a term of endearment, it should have never been used to describe me because it made me feel ugly indeed. No one should be called that, as we are all beautiful in God's eyes; after all, He created us. Psalm 139:14 (NIV) says, "I praise you because I am fearfully and wonderfully made; your works are wonderful. I know that full well." I guess the saying we all know, "sticks and stones may break my bones, but words will never hurt me" is not true after all, because words hurt. They are seeds planted that reap a harvest, good or bad. Sometimes the ones who are closest to us are the ones who hurt us the most. I know she loved me dearly and did not intend to hurt me. As an adult, I recognize I was very impressionable in my youth and I can now reconcile those feelings and be more aware of the words I choose, especially with children.

My grandmother eventually died from diabetes. Despite everything, I choose to remember the good times with her because they far outweigh the bad.

Chapter 9

A Time to Dance

Some people can only imagine taking a trip to Israel, or some are too fearful to make the trek. The day our pastor announced to the congregation that there was going to be a trip to Israel, I knew I had to be part of this journey. I was excited as I always wanted to take this pilgrimage. For many, a trip like this was part of a bucket list, the trip of a lifetime, and here I was being given the opportunity to go. It thrilled me to go with my church because I wanted to walk in the steps that Jesus walked and have the Bible come to life by visiting the various places Jesus traveled.

After service I couldn't wait to get home to share this news with my husband. After discussing with him my desire to go, we decided it would be a great experience and that I should go. I devised a plan to pay for my trip and couldn't wait for the day to come! After I made my initial deposit payment, I had 21 days to purchase a travel insurance plan, which was highly recommended by our tour guides.

Prior to the trip, I was informed who my roommate would be, which was great because it allowed us to meet and get to know each other a bit. We actually met when we attended our Israel kosher lunch four months prior to leaving for our trip. To prepare for our pilgrimage to Israel, one Sunday after service, we all went to a restaurant, Al-Ha'esh Grill, in Bethesda, Maryland to share a meal. There we dined on Middle Eastern dishes, grilled Israeli-style, with side dishes to whet our palates in anticipation of the foods we would eat in the Holy Land.

Eating at this restaurant was a great idea. As someone who loves trying a variety of foods, I really enjoyed sampling the delicacies that were prepared for us. The organizers of the trip, along with the tour company, thought of everything. Besides having us go to dinner, they gave us adapters for our electronics that were compatible with Israel's receptacles. To get us prepared for all the walking we were going to do in Israel, they even arranged trips to the track to get us in shape. Unfortunately, I did not make any of those trips, but I remembered to pack comfortable walking shoes. A very important thing I had to make sure I packed was the medication that I take for my Bipolar I. I would not want to be that far from home and away from my loved ones, my support system, and not have my medication.

When the big day finally arrived for us to leave for Israel, my parents drove me to the airport, where I met up with my roommate and other church members. Our flight left out of Dulles International Airport in Virginia at 11:25 p.m. on Monday, November 4, 2019. We settled in for what was going to be a long 16-hour flight to Tel Aviv, Israel. Before landing in Israel, we had a layover in Istanbul, Turkey, where it took approximately four more hours before we landed in Tel Aviv around 7:20 p.m. the next day (11/5). After going through customs, our representative greeted us and then we met our tour guide and were driven to our hotel, the Ramada Inn & Suites, which was beautifully situated on the shores of the Mediterranean Sea. We received a warm welcome, followed by a reception upon our arrival.

After socializing, my roommate and I went to our room, which came with a balcony that showed a breathtaking view of the city. As tired as we were from the events of the day, my roommate was kind enough to braid my hair. Afterward, we both retired to our plush beds that were waiting for us to jump in after this long day.

This Israel experience was filled with a plethora of activities for us to do, and we could not wait to go on these adventures. Israel is a beautiful place, and we stayed in beautiful hotels like the Ramot Resort Hotel-Sea of Galilee, which was nestled by the magnificent Sea of Galilee! Because we stayed in luxurious hotels, there was great anticipation of all we were going to encounter on this trip. While I would like to share all that I experienced on this pilgrimage, I will share some of the events that significantly impacted me.

One of the most memorable days of the trip was when we started out on a boat ride where we sailed on a boat called "The Jesus Boat" on the Sea of Galilee. This is where a lot of Jesus' ministry took place on the shores of the Sea of Galilee. Four of Jesus' apostles were recruited from these shores. Many miracles took place here, like the walking on the water, calming the storm, the miraculous catching of fish and the feeding of the five thousand people. Jesus' third appearance to his disciples after His resurrection took place here as well. The Sea of Galilee is a fertile place, so I believe this was why Jesus did so much there. As I mentioned earlier, I had my walking on water experience, so to see where it actually happened was inspirational. I was just happy to be in this place that I read about in the Bible as a child.

To add to the excitement of the day, we were all baptized in the Jordan River at Yardenit! After changing into baptismal attire with swim shoes, the baptism took place on the Galilee Baptismal Site on the Jordan River. Being baptized in the Jordan River was a surreal experience because this was actually the place in the Bible where John the Baptist baptized Jesus! It was a rebirth experience for me; it's no longer about me, but Christ. Even though I was baptized before, it felt good to do it again. The feeling of being baptized in this holy place where John the Baptist baptized Jesus was exhilarating. As I waited in line for my turn to go down into the water, I saw the responses of others around me—there were people who wept, praised God after being submerged, and others basked in the moment and remained still. When it was my turn, I was nervous and excited at the same time. After going down in the water and coming back up, I felt refreshed as a new person in Christ and was thankful to God for allowing me to have this experience. I remained still in my spirit and tried to take in the enormity of it all.

This experience went beyond just checking something off my bucket list; it was extremely spiritual. This part of the trip was amazing, a highlight for sure. In reviewing the video, I loved that they captured this memory that we were able to purchase. It captured the baptism of the other church members for us to relish in repeatedly. I even loved the song that was played in the background, "Down in the River to Pray," which is a song often sung at outdoor baptisms, according to Wikipedia. We had a glorious time!

When we all composed ourselves and came down from our high, we left the Jordan River to have lunch at St. Peters Restaurant on the Sea of Galilee and had St. Peters Fish (tilapia). Afterward, we went to the Mount of Beatitudes, where the sermon on the Mount was given from a hill overlooking the Sea of Galilee. We ended the day at the town of Capernaum, where Jesus lived during His Galilean ministry (ref. Matthew 8:1-9). On this day, we truly walked in Jesus' steps. It was simply amazing!

Another highlight for me was when we checked into the Daniel Hotel, Ein Bokek, Dead Sea, perfectly positioned at the lowest place on earth, 1300' below sea level! We finished the night floating in the salty waters of the Dead Sea and the indoor pool (with Dead Sea water) in the hotel. According to "Israel From the Air," a book my mom bought for my grandfather since he could not see Israel in person, was as close as he would get, "The glorious sensation of complete buoyancy has to be experienced to be believed. It is impossible to sink in the Dead Sea; however, it should be noted that drinking the water is not advised. The Dead Sea is a popular health resort, and its mineral, health, and beauty products are marketed all over the world." The products smelled so good, and I couldn't wait to try them all. While I enjoyed floating in the Dead Sea and buying the scented AHAVA beauty products, I couldn't help but think that despite this place being a tourist attraction and beauty mecca, that it is known for receding. This caused me to reflect a bit on my life. I didn't want my life to become stagnant. As I did some self-reflecting, I knew I wanted to continue to flow and move forward and not recede like the Dead Sea or not have life-giving properties. With Bipolar I and not having a relationship with my biological father, I will continue to look ahead and not become stagnant in any area of my life. Overall, when it was all said and done, this day was definitely a memorable moment on the trip for me.

Via Dolorosa is Latin for "Sorrowful Way" and is often translated as "Way of Suffering." It is a processional route in the Old City of Jerusalem and represents the path that Jesus took and was forced by Roman soldiers to walk and carry His cross on the way to his crucifixion. Most of us are familiar with the movie, "The Passion of the Christ" by Mel Gibson and how powerful it was. The Via Dolorosa scene is one of the most poignant scenes in the movie. It depicted the mistreatment of Jesus when he had to carry the cross in the streets of Jerusalem while wearing a thorn-filled crown on His head. This scene was terribly emotional and difficult to watch in the movie. It was so moving that it caused many to bawl seeing what Jesus endured for our sins. It really didn't seem to matter where you were when you watched this scene; it still yielded the same result—bawling!

At one of the former churches I attended, we always had an annual Christmas production (play) that told the story of the life of Christ. We had amazing singers such as gospel singers, Vicki Winans and Lorraine Stancil, who sang Via Dolorosa and after singing it, I don't believe there was ever a dry eye in the building. It was always so moving as we watched the actor emulate Jesus carrying that cross and being beaten and mistreated just for us.

As we walked the steps of Jesus, Via Dolorosa, on this day, it was difficult walking this path. This was actually where the Game of King was played with the crowning of thorns, the torturing of Jesus, and where they put the arm part of the cross on his shoulders and led Him out. It was here where one member of our group was caught up in the emotion of it all and wept. It was so moving.

After this emotional tug at your heartstrings experience, we went to one of the most sacred places in Israel, the Western Wall, which is known as Judaism's most sacred site. Now this was a pivotal point in the trip for me, as I found it to be such a spiritual and intimate time with God. According to The Western Wall Heritage Foundation's brochure this is "The most visited site in Israel and is the only fragment of the Great Temple to survive the Roman destruction. It is said that the Divine Presence has never departed from the Western Wall. People from all over the world converge there, to see, feel, pray, and to wedge notes, requests, and pleas between its timeless stones."

Knowing this, I placed my prayers in the wall that I had written out for my family and friends. Every nook and cranny had written prayers in them already, so I had to climb on some plastic chairs to find a space to put mine! Once I did that and prayed at the wall, I left from where I was standing/praying and noticed that when people left the wall, they did not turn their backs to the wall as I unknowingly did. But we later found out, after asking, that you back away from the wall by still facing it and once at a distance away from it you could turn around. This is done in reverence and awe of the presence of God. This was EPIC! To revere the presence of God. To be in the presence of God. To see others in reverence of God. Priceless!

This pilgrimage was truly humbling and eye-opening. I felt closer to God and feel that I developed a greater intimacy with Him just from this trip. I hope at some point I will have the opportunity to go back again because it was so much to take in within 10 days. We woke up around 6 a.m. each day to eat breakfast and board the buses and we didn't get back to the hotels until about 6 p.m. We changed hotels four times, so we had to have our bags packed to load on and off the buses at each destination. Even though the weather was warm, we had to dress in layers to be prepared for weather fluctuations, and if we visited a holy site, we needed to be dressed more modestly.

There were so many highlights to this trip, but the major theme that resonated with me was walking in the steps and places that Jesus and other Bible characters walked and worked. I cannot put into words the magnitude of this trip. I felt a closeness and connection with God with each day's experience. It was a spiritual awakening, and I wanted to be a part of the service of serving others as Jesus did. My heart's desire is that others will consider making the trip to the Holy Land as it is an experience like none other. It will change your life!

Nothing illustrated for me more clearly the awesomeness of God than when we overlooked the city in Israel while Pastor Kevin preached on the Trinity Broadcasting Network (TBN). This was a showstopper! I was so proud to see him give a sermon on this television station that's viewed by many worldwide. He preached a powerful message titled, "Do you Remember?" from the book of Zechariah 2:1-13. The title of the sermon was so relevant. Yes, I will always remember this trip! I will remember traveling in Jesus' footsteps. I will remember my baptism in the Jordan River. I will remember floating on the Dead Sea and even riding a camel. I will remember all of this! More than a check off the bucket list, this was a memory that will last a lifetime. I thank God for the opportunity. This certainly was a time to rejoice; indeed, a time to dance! To God be the glory for the wonderful things He has done.

My Trip to Israel

The Pilgrimage

Conclusion

My life has come full circle. You see me at one of my lowest points in the beginning of the book where I went on a high school ski trip at 17 where I lost touch with reality, to a mountaintop experience with a trip to Israel over 30 years later! I am a survivor. My life is a true testament that you can live a full life despite having a mental disorder diagnosis. To some, having a mental disorder can be crippling mentally. It can cause you to limit yourself in your thoughts where you believe you cannot do certain things based on your diagnosis. Bipolar I, with its polar opposite moods, can interrupt your life and the life of those around you. It can even be difficult to be in relationships. It requires being surrounded by people who are patient and understanding. I have had my share of trials since my diagnosis, but I am an overcomer!

Bipolar I could have knocked me down at certain points in my life, but it has not knocked me out. From having manic episodes, marrying and having children (who are well-adjusted and productive in society), maintaining a long and successful career, receiving many accolades over my thirty-year career (e.g., winning trips and awards), enduring family hurts that could have triggered me and caused me to have mental breakdowns, and then taking the trip of a lifetime, prove that if properly managed, someone diagnosed with Bipolar I can live a normal life.

Being diligent and remaining on the medication that was right for me allowed me to function just like the next person. If I can do it, others can do the same! I am a living example that you do not have to live a life feeling bound. By having the right people in your corner, a great support system (i.e., God, family, therapist/counselor, psychiatrist/doctors), demonstrating extreme self-care, and by God's grace, you can live a rewarding life with Bipolar I or any other mental disorder.

Romans 12:15 (AMP) says, "Rejoice with those who rejoice [sharing others' joy], and weep with those who weep [sharing others' grief]." Writing this book is a call to action for others to be encouraged in knowing that they can also persevere, despite a mental illness. I rejoice as I gained my voice and was able to change my narrative. I want to help others find their joy and turn their weeping into rejoicing. I pray something you read in this book will bless you. Be encouraged and remember Philippians 4:13 (KJV) and know that "I (you) can do all things through Christ which strengtheneth me (you). To God be the glory for the marvelous things He has done and will continue to do in our lives!

About the Author

Nikki J. Collier is a distinguished alumna of Towson State University (now Towson University) where she graduated with a Bachelor of Arts degree in Mass Communications. She is a loving wife, devoted mother, and a proud, young grandmother. With a career spanning over three decades, she has made a significant impact in the fields of radio and TV sales and marketing. Nikki's expertise in branding and marketing has led her to serve as an invaluable advisor to many organizations through her work. In addition to her professional achievements, she is an active and dedicated member of her church, The Shepherd's House International Christian Church in Upper Marlboro, Md, where her passion for evangelism shines through. What truly sets her apart is her unparalleled attention to detail and commitment in everything she does. Furthermore, she has taken on a vital role in the community, having initiated a mental health ministry in partnership with her church. Under her leadership, this ministry features an annual forum of experts in the field, aimed at bridging the gap between the African American Church and mental health awareness. Beyond her career and community involvement, Nikki is now a first-time author, which allows her to share her insights and knowledge with the world. Her multifaceted journey is a testament to her passion, dedication, and unwavering commitment to excellence.

To contact Nikki Collier: nikkicollier@girdupyourmind.com

References

Chapter 1: A Time to Lose

1. Today.com July 24, 2020 "What is bipolar disorder? Expert explains misunderstood condition, symptoms" by Kerry Breen
https://www.today.com/health/what-bipolar-disorder-symptoms-causes-mood-disorders-t187761
2. Special Time Edition Mental Health A New Understanding-Article "Finding The Right Words" by David Bjerklie
3. "Paradigms Lost" by Stuart and co-authors Norman Sartorius and Julio Arbeoleda-Florez
4. "Processing your diagnosis through the stages of grief" December 17, 2022, Lung Foundation Australia
https://lungfoundation.com.au/blog/processing-your-diagnosis-through-the-stages-of grief/#:~:text=You%20may%20grieve%20the%20loss%20of%20your%20health%2C,common%20being%20denial%2C%20anger%2C%20bargaining%2C%20depression%2C%20and%20acceptance.

Chapter 2: A Time to Be Born

1. "Definition of Pre-Eclampsia" by Medical Editor: Charles Patrick Davis, MD, PhD MedicineNet
https://www.medicinenet.com/pre-eclampsia/definition.htm

2. Sparkling Gems from the Greek by Rick Renner Vol. 1 "Never Forget That You Are More Than a Conqueror!" January 20th (page 38)

Chapter 3: A Time to Die

1. Merriam-Webster Dictionary-the word "die" https://www.merriam-webster.com/dictionary/die
2. The Free Dictionary- the word "die" https://www.thefreedictionary.com/die

Chapter 4: A Time to Plant

1. Merriam-Webster Dictionary the word "plant" https://www.merriam-webster.com/dictionary/plant
2. Some content taken from Matthew Henry's Commentary Volume 5 Matthew to John, Copyright 1991 Used by permission of Hendrickson Rose Publishing Group, represented by Tyndale House Publishers. All rights reserved. Matthew14:22-33 pg. 164, pg. 167
3. Wikipedia "Luther's Small Catechism" https://en.wikipedia.org/wiki/Luther%27s_Small_Catechism
4. "The Parable of a Valuable Pearl" Posted by Brian Barrier | Oct 7, 2019 | https://blueridgechristiannews.com/the-parable-of-a-valuable-pearl/

Chapter 5: A Time to Pluck Up That Which is Planted

1. "The God Who Stoops" by Joel Osteen

2. "What is Peripartum Depression (formerly Postpartum)?" https://www.psychiatry.org/patients-families/postpartum-depression/what-is-postpartum-depression

3. "Postpartum Psychosis" https://www.postpartum.net/learn-more/postpartum-sychosis/#:~:text=In%20her%20psychotic%20state%2C%20the,going%20through%20psychosis%20is%20imperative.

Chapter 6: A Time to Heal

1. Merriam- Webster Dictionary-the word "heal" https://www.merriam-webster.com/dictionary/heal

2. "Obi-Wan Kenobi A Jedi's Return" (Documentary on Disney+)

3. "The Five Love Languages: How to Express Heartfelt Commitment to Your Mate" by Gary Chapman, Moody Publishers, Copyright 1992, 1995, 2004 Chapter 5 Love Language #2: Quality Time pg. 64, pg.69

4. Census Bureau: Higher Percentage of Black Children Live with Single Mothers https://afro.com/census-bureau-higher-percentage-black-children-live-single-mothers/

Chapter 7: A Time to Breakdown

1. "Overcomer" (film) by Alex and Stephen Kendrick

2. "Run Your Race" by Pastor Kevin Matthews

3. Sparkling Gems from the Greek by Rick Renner Vol. 1 "Gird Up the Loins of Your Mind!" June 27 (page 445)

4. Let's Talk About Him w/ Tammie Padillo New Beginnings Night of Prayer "Girding Up the Lions of Your Mind" Evangelist Anita Bryant

5. Joel Osteen "Fight For Your Future"

Chapter 8: A Time to Weep

1. Dictionary.com the word "weep" https://www.dictionary.com/browse/weep

Chapter 9: A Time to Dance

1. Wikipedia "Via Dolorosa" https://en.wikipedia.org/wiki/Via_Dolorosa

2. Israel Advantage Tours 10-day Spiritual Journey of a Lifetime through the Holy Land November 4-13, 2019 Suggested Sites Itinerary

3. "Israel from the air" by Itamar Grinberg pg.33 VMB Publishers, 1998, 2007

4. Via Dolorosa-Holy Land Guides-Shalom Advertising

5. The Western Wall -The Western Wall Heritage Foundation

6. Wikipedia "Sea of Galilee" https://en.wikipedia.org/wiki/Sea_of_Galilee